VIOLENT SUNDAYS

Bob Chandler
and Norm Chandler Fox

A FIRESIDE BOOK
Published by Simon & Schuster, Inc.
NEW YORK

To Marilyn and Marisa, my lifelong teammates, and to Justin, who was just picked up on waivers . . . and with special thanks to my parents

B.C.

For my partner-in-life, Loreen, whose love has been an inspiration and whose faith in me has never waivered . . . and for my twin, Jeri, whose generous spirit and courage enriched all of us who knew her.

N.C.F.

A Pegasus Production
Pegasus is a division of the RGA Publishing Group, Inc.

Copyright © 1984 by RGA Publishing Group, Inc.

A Fireside Book
Published by Simon & Schuster, Inc.
Simon & Schuster Building
Rockefeller Center
1230 Avenue of the Americas
New York, New York 10020

FIRESIDE and colophon are registered trademarks of Simon & Schuster, Inc.

Designed by Stanley S. Drate/Folio Graphics Co. Inc.

Manufactured in the United States of America

Printed and bound by Fairfield Graphics

10 9 8 7 6 5 4 3 2 1

Library of Congress Cataloging in Publication Data

Chandler, Bob.
  Violent Sundays.

  "A Fireside book."
  1. Chandler, Bob. 2. Football players—United States—
Biography. 3. National Football League. I. Fox,
Norm Chandler. II. Title.
GV939.C48A38 1984   796.332'092'4 [B] 84-5316
ISBN: 0-671-47460-X

CONTENTS

1

The Injury That Almost Cost Me My Life— Looking Back

To give your all at that moment,
No regard for consequences.
Having mind free from doubt,
Body knowing self-respect.
What price is this duty owed
To yourself and no one else.
Mirrors show what eyes can't see—
Pride clears the picture and fills the need.

—BOB CHANDLER
1975—Niagara University
Training Camp

Please, God, I don't want to die! I mean, I'm only thirty-two, for Christ's sake. According to the actuarial tables given out by insurance salesmen, I'm supposed to have about forty more good years ahead of me. I just want to grow old with my wife, make a fuss over our grandchildren, and even collect a few social security checks.

Those were the kinds of thoughts that spun through my head as I lay within a tiny cubicle in the intensive care unit at St. Luke's Hospital in Denver. Thank God, Donald Fink, the Raiders' team physician, was standing near the entrance of the ICU talking to some other doctors. Had I not seen his familiar face, I would've felt like I was in a foreign country. It was painful to realize that I could die at any time surrounded almost totally by strangers. And most chilling of all was the thought that when you die, you have to do it all by yourself.

To ease my terror, I fantasized having my wife, Marilyn, and my four-year-old daughter, Marisa, at my bedside along with my parents and two sisters. At first, it was a nice fantasy, with the members of my family telling me, in turn, how much I meant to them, but slowly they all started to get pissed off about my life being wasted by something as inconsequential as football. Clearing that scene from my head, I opened my eyes and stared at the machine that was monitoring my heartbeat and became aware of the undulating recording it made and the beep sound that signified I was still alive. The small screen read 135 beats per minute, which scared the hell out of me. Of all the painful and crippling injuries I had sustained throughout my football career, at least I knew in every instance what was wrong with me. Now, no one seemed to know what was causing my body to self-destruct. Maybe if I stared at the monitoring screen long enough, I could send the numbers plummeting down to normal through sheer force of will. It didn't work. It should've. Then I pondered about what a sad word is "should." I was thinking of all the times I should've told my wife how much she meant to me, should've helped out and kept in closer touch with my Buffalo Bills buddy, Tony Greene, should've spent more time watching my baby daughter turn into a little girl. Maybe I even should've worn more protection playing football.

A sudden wave of nausea caused my body to shake, and I began to gag until a nurse took the oxygen mask off my face. She mumbled something about it being a lousy day for me. I suppose any day that you die turns out to be your lousiest. I started laughing at the absurdity of what I was going through. I couldn't understand why my luck had suddenly run out. I thought about the last few days and realized that the whole goddamned trip to Denver was jinxed almost as if somebody was trying to tell me something. . . .

We were assembling at the Oakland airport for the first game of the 1981–82 season, and we were in great spirits. We had every right to be happy as hell since we were crowned world champions at the Super Bowl a mere eight months earlier. But the Oakland Raiders didn't look like world champions; instead, we appeared to the disinterested observer like the alumni attending a class reunion at San Quentin.

After boarding our chartered DC-8, we all were surprised and disappointed when we realized that Al LoCasale, the man who runs the football operation off the field, had replaced all the regular stewardesses who had flown with us to all our out-of-town games for the past two years. We couldn't figure out why Al would do such a thing unless he thought that some of the team members were fraternizing a little too frequently with the ladies in blue. Unfortunately, Al forgot to take into consideration just how superstitious all of us were about wanting to fly with the same crew that had accompanied us to our greatest victories. Worse still, the new stewardesses seemed to have just graduated at the top of their class from in-flight school.

Believing that these uptight ladies would loosen up once we were airborne, the Raiders began their usual ritual of turning the plane's cabin into their own private social club. My teammates casually ignored the seat-belt sign as many of them lounged across entire rows of seats while others were busily pushing down the backs of seats to create makeshift tables for some serious card-playing. As the aircraft taxied down the runway, the new stewardesses went crazy trying to make these naughty 260-pounders obey the rules. At the end of the runway, the plane stopped, and over the intercom the pilot said, "I don't know where you guys learned your manners, but this aircraft must fly under federal regulations. So, we're not taking off until every one of you is sitting upright in your seat with your belts fastened!" That announcement was followed by shouts of "Fuck him and his seat belts," and the plane just sat there for a half hour until we all reluctantly decided to play by the rules. However, our need for independence surged forth once we were in the air, and before the seat-belt sign went off, we proceeded to move around and adjust the seats to our particular needs. The uniformed ladies decided that the only way they could keep their sanity was by ignoring us. I was glad they followed their instincts to leave us alone, since I always felt that football players traveling together were similar to soldiers on a troop train or sailors on a battleship. All of us were going off to our own wars, and therefore we should be allowed a truce to do our thing. But I felt sorry for the stewardesses who weren't ready for the abuse we gave them. One young lady spent the rest of the trip sobbing in the back of the plane.

Somewhere over central Utah, our plane hit unexpected turbulence, forcing the captain to turn on the seat-belt sign again. When no one heeded it, our leader came back on the intercom with the warning that he'd land the plane in Salt Lake City in ten minutes if we didn't behave. Thinking that we'd all get fined if he made a forced landing, we reluctantly gave in.

Being a white-knuckle flyer, I was getting upset about the entire flight. Just outside of Denver, the plane hit some thunderclouds that caused us to bounce like Ping-Pong balls until we landed, and I felt certain that the pilot aimed at those clouds just to teach us a lesson. Driving into town from the airport, I began to get a feeling in the pit of my stomach that the flight was merely a prelude of things to come this weekend.

Part of this weekend was planned as a small reunion for some people I've known for a good part of my life. My best friend, Jay Bligh, and his wife, Marie, had flown out from Los Angeles to see me and the game, and we all had dinner with another good friend, John Grant (who formerly played for the Denver Broncos), and his wife, Minica. Dining at a fancy restaurant, I noticed two gorgeous women next to us who were drinking their dates under the table. I kept staring, trying to determine what was wrong with the picture, when suddenly one of the women opened her mouth and threw up all over her date and all over the table. After witnessing that, I couldn't eat very much, and I kept wondering what other grotesque events were in store for this weekend.

Back in my hotel that night, I couldn't fall asleep. A feeling of fear began to take hold of me, and I kept believing that although I was in excellent physical shape, I just wasn't mentally ready to play tomorrow. Having never experienced that feeling before a game, I was already beginning to get spooked by it.

Not to worry, I kidded myself, as I entered the locker room the next day and started going through my pregame ritual of medication. First, I got a shot of Xylocaine in my foot to numb my chronic condition of Morton's Neuroma, which could flare up and impede my running. Next, I took some Indocin, a very strong antiinflammatory drug that cannot be taken more than two days at a time without certain side effects. Instinctively, I knew how hard the drug was on my system, but I felt it was a small price to pay for getting through the game.

After getting dressed, the entire team sat quietly for a few moments either listening to music or meditating; the purpose of this was to "psych" yourself up to perform on the field. While sitting, I realized how exhausted I felt and blamed it on the mile-high altitude of Denver. I also noticed that those fearful feelings of the night before hadn't dissipated; however, they felt more like stage fright than fears of something happening to me. I decided I needed some Benzedrine to perk me up. Since our trainers aren't permitted to dispense "bennies," I got one from one of the players. There was always someone on the team who had some, and since this was the beginning of the season, all supplies were up. I never had second thoughts about ingesting ten milligrams of Benzedrine since such a mild dose rarely did more than temporarily rev up my energy.

After running out on the field, I began to go through warm-ups, and I kept thinking that I had to get my mind under control.

I had experienced similar uneasy symptoms before during warm-ups, but they disappeared after kickoff when I started concentrating on the game. After the game started, I still felt peculiar. It was a surreal feeling that I had gotten outside my body and was watching myself playing in the game.

It was during the second quarter that I was blocking Denver's Louie Wright (All-Pro defensive back), who got a cramp in his leg and went out after our second down. I remember telling our quarterback, Jim Plunkett, that Louie Wright was hurt and they were bringing in a new cornerback, Perry Smith. Plunkett felt this was a good time to throw the ball, and so he called a quick-out, which is a six-yard pass to the outside. As the ball was coming to me, I turned around and reached out to catch it. Usually on a quick-out, I'll go out of bounds after the catch, but this time I planted my feet within the boundaries, and as I stretched to grab the ball, my midsection was exposed. Perry Smith was running full speed with his body low and hit me right in the stomach with his face. When I realize how tough it is to break a face mask, I find it particularly awesome that the impact from the blow tore up his face mask. I was stunned and fell out of bounds while still holding onto the ball. I was laying on my back with my feet up in the air, and I remember tossing the ball over my head in disgust. I couldn't breathe for a few seconds, and yet, it didn't feel like the wind was knocked out of me. Instead, I felt as if my insides were paralyzed all the way up to my throat. Mustering what strength I had, I got up and slowly walked to the bench while Morris Bradshaw took my place on the field. Sitting on the bench for a few minutes, I began to get very dizzy and actually talked myself into believing it was the altitude. The trainers told me to go over to the oxygen machine, and after breathing in pure oxygen for ten minutes, I began to feel that everything was settling down inside.

Because it was the season's first game, I desperately wanted to catch some balls, so I went back in the game with just a few minutes to play before half time. Every time I ran a pattern, I was fighting just to stand up and had to open my eyes wider with force just to keep things from moving around for me. The dizziness came back and I began to feel bloated in my gut.

At half time, I was examined in our training room, and the consensus was that my bloated feeling came from being hit hard in the abdomen, which caused my stomach to go into spasms. My blood pressure and heart rate weren't checked primarily because so many guys get hit in the stomach, back and chest all the time that it usually doesn't warrant a more detailed examination. Interestingly, I was asked if I had any pain in my shoulder, which would indicate a spleen problem. There was no shoulder pain, and although I still felt slightly nauseous and dizzy, I wanted to continue playing in the third quarter. In retrospect, that turned out to be a catastrophic choice.

I was getting progressively dizzier with each pattern I ran. The Broncos seemed to have multiplied, since every player in my line of vision had a twin brother standing next to him. Two Louie Wrights had replaced Perry Smith, and when I bumped into both of them on my way to our huddle, I apologized, saying that I was so dizzy I couldn't see straight. In the huddle, instead of worrying what the fuck was wrong with me, I was actually worrying about the fact that Louie Wright now knew I was a complete pushover. The nausea was getting worse, and I decided that I would get out of the game after catching one more pass.

Going down to the ten-yard line, I ran a cross pattern. Plunkett threw the ball low, forcing me to reach out, and as I caught the ball, I could see peripherally that I was about to be hit. Thank God, I had the presence of mind to spin in order to protect my stomach area, and I was brought down with a blow to my hip. Had I gotten hit in the stomach, I might have died right there on the field. This time, it was a massive struggle to get up, but I was determined to do it alone, since I've always hated those guys with relatively minor injuries who allow themselves to be carried off the field. I mean, it's really embarrassing to see the same guy playing in the next quarter after the stretcher carries him off like a fallen hero.

The bright September sun was in my eyes as I slowly staggered toward the bench. The stadium kept moving in and out of focus while simultaneously spinning like a top. By now, I was falling down every few steps, and I honestly didn't think I'd make it to the team doctor standing ten yards away.

Dr. Donald Fink is truly one of the funniest guys I know. Having a physical examination done by him is like being entertained by a very original stand-up comedian. Besides being the official team doctor, Don has a medical practice and an investment-counseling business on the side. I often wondered how such an entertaining guy would react in an emergency, and I was soon to learn that he was phenomenal.

After noting that my color was a ghastly white, he put me on the ground with my feet up on the bench. Attaching an intravenous solution of plasma to my arm, Fink surmised I was bleeding internally, since my systolic blood pressure fell from a normal 120 to an alarming 70 while my heart was pounding away at 140 beats per minute. After ordering an ambulance to meet us at the stadium's entrance, Fink and the trainers gently placed me on a gurney and put cold towels on my forehead. I must've looked like death warmed over as I was being wheeled past my teammates, since the expressions on their faces told me that they were scared shitless I wasn't going to survive. The television cameras also picked up my not so glorious exit, with the announcer sympathetically mentioning how unusual it was to see a player already hooked up to an IV while being wheeled off the playing field. Knowing that my parents were watching the game in California, I actually started worrying about something happening to my mother from the shock of seeing a close-up of her only son looking like he was relaxing in Death's waiting room.

We had to wait a few moments for the ambulance, and as I was lying beneath the stands, I looked up and saw a man motioning to me. He yelled, "Hey, Chandler, looks like you won't be catching any more passes today!" Fink roared and said, "Must be a Bronco fan, Bobby." I quietly replied, "No shit?"

Before getting into the ambulance, I felt very frightened. It was like being a little kid who has gotten lost and now realizes that he may never find his way home. I was in a strange city and going to an unknown hospital filled with specialists I'd never heard of before.

When the ambulance got moving, Fink told the driver to take us to the nearest hospital, and by a stroke of luck, he took us instead to St. Luke's Hospital, which happens to be one of the best in the city. During the ride, my blood pressure was fluctuating between 60 and 70, and although Donald Fink kept making jokes, I could tell by the fact that he was drenched in sweat that he was as scared as I was. With all this going on, I was reassured seeing Jay Bligh and his wife sitting in the front seat of the ambulance.

In the hospital's emergency room, I endured having an oxygen mask applied, which caused me to gag violently, forcing them to remove the mask, which induced my losing consciousness. This horrible round-robin continued until they placed me on the x-ray table and cut off my uniform. After taking pictures, the emergency staff kept asking me where the pain was. Oddly enough, I felt a slight soreness in my abdomen, but no real pain. I suppose it's the mentality I acquired after playing eleven years of professional ball. I've always made up my mind that I wouldn't give in to pain. If I became injured, I would only feel it for an instant, and then I would continue to play unless I was totally incapacitated. Thus, my psychological acceptance of pain as an integral part of my profession often helped to modify whatever was hurting me.

The x-rays proved inconclusive and the source of the internal bleeding wasn't identified. All of a sudden, I felt my entire body tingling, and I broke out in a cold sweat before passing out. They tilted the x-ray table to lower my head and raise my feet, and I remained in that position for a while until I became semiconscious.

Meanwhile, one of Denver's finest internists, Gerald Kirshenbaum, had been watching the game on television, and had an unsettling intuition that I would soon be visiting his hospital after seeing me being rolled out of the stadium. When I was told that Dr. Kirshenbaum was on his way over to see me, they could've told me it was Bo Derek, for all I cared. My last blood pressure reading hovered at 30, and I knew that there weren't that many more numbers left on the blood pressure meter.

After being raced up to the intensive care unit, I noticed that I was being wheeled into cubicle #13. Donald Fink made me smile at the irony of this being the only cubicle available. "Yeah," I mumbled, "this one must have the highest turnover rate." I was immediately hooked up to a battery of machines which recorded in lights, sounds, digits and graphs all of my vital signs. I wondered which machine would start blinking if I happened to get an erection—if that was still possible.

I liked Kirshenbaum instantly because he wasn't one of those scalpel-happy guys who operate first and ask questions later. In fact, he told me that exploratory surgery would be his last resort, since that would probably keep me out of football for the entire year. If I had more strength, I would've gone into a long speech about how unimportant the game of football had suddenly become to me. All I wanted now was for Somebody Upstairs to exercise His option and renew my lease on life.

Kirshenbaum wanted to wait until my vital signs stabilized before making any decisions for treatment. Meanwhile, he was going to collect the ultrasound team to obtain a more definitive picture of just what was going on inside of me.

My thoughts about this bizarre weekend had come full circle, and now I had nothing else to do but wait and stare at the heartbeat-monitoring screen. During moments of intense anxiety, I've often had childlike magical thoughts composed of my doing something which, in turn, would cause something else to happen. My current brainstorm was that if I kept an eye on the heartbeat machine, I would stay alive. Not terribly logical, but at the time, it made incredible sense to me. After a full five minutes of my undivided attention, I noticed that my heartrate was beginning to slow down. My God, I thought, I'm curing myself! My euphoria lasted approximately one minute, and then I started getting panicky as I watched the monitor go from 115 down to

90 in seconds; then, it went all the way down to 45 beats per minute, which tripped off a warning buzzer. As I started to pass out, the screen registered 30, and I learned later that a shot of adrenaline was used to revive me. By this time, my blood pressure was so low that they couldn't get an accurate reading on it.

A few minutes later, my vital signs stabilized again, but we all knew that this was only temporary. Kirshenbaum introduced me to the ultrasound team, who proceeded to place something over my midsection, turn out the lights, and operate the machine, which projected a picture of my internal organs on a screen. No one spoke for a few moments until one of the doctors uttered, "Good Lord, there's over a gallon of blood just floating in his abdomen." Kirshenbaum turned on the lights and looked at me almost apologetically, saying, "Bob, we've no choice but to go in!"

Even though I was scared out of my mind, I gave the impression of inner peace as I methodically told Don Fink to call my wife, tell her about the surgery, and insist that she not fly to Denver. I really wanted to spare her the anxiety of being in a strange city and the horror of not knowing if she'd return to California as a widow. Afterward Don phoned my parents to tell them about the operation. He told me that my dad was already packing and determined to make the last Denver flight out of LAX (Los Angeles). I guess no one could tell my dad not to come once he made up his mind.

As they were preparing the operating room, a nurse put a tube in my nose which went all the way down to my stomach, and I was given blood intravenously to keep my levels up. Suddenly, like an apparition, one of the hospital nuns appeared by my bed and asked me to sign some releases. As I was doing that, she asked me if I wanted to see a priest. Despite the fact that I was barely conscious, I got pissed off and told her to leave me alone. She was about as welcome at that moment as my insurance agent would have been if he was coming to tell me that my life insurance policy had expired.

As I was being wheeled into the operating room, I saw my

friends, Jay and Marie Bligh and John Grant, in the corridor. They all wished me luck, but I could see terror in their eyes because I looked more dead than alive.

The gigantic operating-room light blinded me momentarily when I was first wheeled in. One nurse began prepping my abdomen while another started strapping me down to the table. I saw Kirshenbaum standing next to me and holding up his gloved hands. He looked like Moses about to receive the Commandments. With my one free hand, I grabbed one of his and said, "I don't care about football. In fact, I don't care if I ever play again. I just want to live!" The last thing I remember hearing before I started becoming unconscious was Dr. Kirshenbaum muttering, "Nurse, get me some clean gloves."

And as I blacked out slowly, I blocked the thought of my never waking up with thoughts of my entire football career. My mind raced back to my senior year in high school and the dilemma of choosing the right football scholarship. Football had always been one of my life's greatest pleasures. It was ironic that playing a game could become a matter of life or death.

2

From Whittier to the Rose Bowl—In the Beginning

"Winning is not everything . . . it's the only thing."
Bullshit, excellence is the objective of this game.
We must not lose sight of this or we no longer have a sport.

—Bob Chandler
1977—Buffalo, New York

I never thought I was someone special. But I sure tried to be somewhat of an individual. Coming from a family where no one was really hooked on athletics, my love of sports grew all by itself. I had very little desire for watching sports; my driving need was to be strictly a participant.

One of my life's great blessings was being raised in Whittier, California—a fiercely middle-class community on the unfashionable side of Los Angeles and full of hardworking churchgoing people. A year-round mild climate pulled me outdoors most of the time to play football, baseball, even basketball on cement courts, and to compete in track, which I loved most of all. I remember making the varsity baseball team as a fourteen-year-old freshman, but when I realized that I wouldn't start my first year, I unceremoniously quit to go out for track. I guess my basic instincts fought against my being a team player, since nothing satisfied me more than competing individually in track.

Going to Whittier High School was another blessing because the coaches encouraged athletes to go out for as many different sports as possible. Today, too many high schools have accelerated football programs where the coaches promote the notion that football *must* be an all-year endeavor. The results are deadly. Since the athletes are not encouraged to go out for other sports, their only off-season recreation is lifting weights. After four or five years of concentrating only on football, some of these guys just burn out halfway through college.

Although I liked track better, there was something that attracted me to football. Being sort of a loner, I was best suited to the position of wide receiver. Here was the best of all worlds—I could perform as a team player while still retaining my independence as I split out from the rest of the guys. Essentially, I could engage in a one-on-one duel with the defensive back.

But there were other reasons that propelled me into football. At the risk of sounding like a borderline schizophrenic, I'll concede that football permitted me the luxury of dividing my personality in half. I've always considered myself to be a quiet, laid-back, reserved kind of guy, and basically very shy. Football gave me a tough guy identity and convinced people that I was special. Therefore, I could lean on my ability to play football to carry me through any situation. Ironically, people who meet me for the first time are dumbfounded to learn that I've been in professional football all these years. I'm usually told that I'm not big enough or that I don't look like the kind of a guy who could take such a constant beating. Most amazing is how many people project their own shortcomings on an atypical-looking athlete like myself. Belligerent, beery-eyed men have come up to me in bars and restaurants saying something like, "I'm the same size as you, and if only I hadn't hurt my knee in high school, I could be out there every Sunday instead of a shit like you!"

Perhaps, I'm a slow learner, but it didn't really dawn on me until my senior year in high school that football had turned me into a special commodity. In the fall of that year, I felt that I had really arrived when I received a scholarship offer from Whittier College. It didn't matter that the school was practically in my backyard or that I'd probably be going to college with the same group from high school. When one of the football coaches from Whittier invited me to his apartment for dinner, I was dazzled beyond belief, thinking that I had finally made the big time!

One month later, I felt I'd hit the jackpot when Brigham Young University offered to fly me out at their expense just to take a look at the school. I was too embarrassed to tell them that this was the first time I'd ever been outside of California, as well as on a plane. After receiving a warm welcome from their coach, Tommy Hudspeth, I was shown such incredible facilities as an indoor practice field and was told that being a non-Mormon could work to my advantage. Regardless, I was ready to convert that same night after being fixed up with a beautiful Mormon freshman. She was so persuasive that I signed a letter of intent to go to Brigham Young. (Many years later, when I was in the NFL, I heard fabulous stories about the exotic women that numerous schools trotted out in order to snare some unwitting athlete. Since I wasn't that highly recruited, I missed out on most of the good stuff.)

I received an inquiry from the Air Force Academy, but I felt I'd be wasting their time and the taxpayers' dollars to look at the school, since my being color-blind would prevent me from learning how to fly. And, needless to say, I wasn't looking forward to going out with a freshman cadet.

My high school coaches, Vic Lopez and Don Kelley, took it upon themselves to phone the University of Southern California. They had contacted USC only once before, and that was regarding George Buehler, who ultimately was a top college player at Stanford and went on to play with the Oakland Raiders. The athletic department at USC knew that Vic wouldn't call unless he was on to some real talent, which prompted their sending one of their scouts, Rod Humenick (who's now the offensive line coach for the Kansas City Chiefs), to watch me in action. Humenick had to improvise because it was winter and I was playing basketball. In this particular game, the opposing team's coach sent in a guy to get me out of the game. As I went in for a layup, this kid punched me right below the eye and knocked me against the wall. Not knowing that I would later need six stitches to close my wound, I got up and naturally fought back (which Humenick loved), had them put a bandage over my eye, and started to play again after having missed about one minute of the game (which made Humenick positively ecstatic). USC decided I'd make a great defensive back, since I demonstrated how thick-skulled I was—having been clobbered by this guy, and willingly come back for more.

There must be some sort of underground network in Los Angeles, because as soon as USC showed interest in me, UCLA got jealous and decided to take a look also. After I spent a day getting the grand tour of UCLA, I received a letter stating that on second thought they didn't think I was ready for big-time college football. They suggested I enroll in a junior college, and they would evaluate my performance later. I was a bit embarrassed and wondered how many guys got led down the primrose path to junior college only to be forgotten when it came time to reevaluate two years later.

I was a little wary when I was told I was accepting the very last of the twenty-some scholarships that USC gave out that year. Knowing that USC had great second- and third- string players, I worried most about not having a chance to ever play, but Rod Humenick swore that the school looked upon me as a sleeper and expected I would become one of their top players in a very short time. (I'm sure they say that to everybody.) Putting the school's best foot forward, Rod invited me and Vic Lopez to the USC–Notre Dame game with the intention of introducing me to John McKay and all the players after the game. However, after the Trojans got beaten 51 to 0, I figured it would be a little anticlimactic for me to go in the locker room and shake their hands, so we decided against it.

Entering USC was a very exciting time for me, since I'd always wanted to go to college and never dreamed that a school would pay me to do it. Although I would never admit it at the time, I was always in awe when I passed by the statue of Tommy Trojan in the middle of the campus. The university's athletic department was very attentive to the athletes' wants and needs, but going to class was probably never policed as much as it should have been. You never forgot that you were brought to USC because you could play football, and as long as you stayed eligible, your private life was pretty much your own business. For me, this was perfect.

I paid for my books and went to all my classes. Majoring in finance, even though I was unable to put in very much study time, I had a C average. I felt it was very important for me to graduate. Since both my parents had always worked hard and done very well without the benefit of college, there was no real guidance they could give me. So I had to feel my own way. Being somewhat insecure about my own athletic ability and wondering how long it would last, I drove myself to at least get a decent education at USC.

Unfortunately for so many college football players, they begin to distort the importance football has in their lives. They rarely attend classes, never buy any books, and usually don't graduate. They take just enough courses to stay eligible with the help of cooperative teachers and administrators. Generally players have very little connection with the university other than spending the four most productive years of their lives doing nothing except trying to play football. Even today, the system hasn't changed much; only about 35 percent of professional football players are college graduates. I'm not getting on a soapbox to preach about the virtues of getting a degree, but the real tragedy is how hermetically sealed-off you can become. By going to a minimum of classes, you can lose such fundamental skills as relating to people and to new situations. The system foments a closed circle wherein football players spend most of their time with other football players. They all come to expect that any obstacles or hurdles in life will be solved for them, and they usually are. If they don't want to stand in line to register, they can always ask a go-for who'll do it for them. Rather than walk a half mile to class after parking in the student parking lot, they will park illegally in every red zone on campus, knowing that the ticket will be taken care of by somebody, and I was no exception to this life-style.

I must confess that all of us were very much aware of the fact that we were participating in big-time college football, which put pressure on us to perform brilliantly every Saturday. And after busting their asses every afternoon with practice, most of the guys were too exhausted physically to spend much time studying. For myself, it was hard as hell to crack the books at night. Thankfully, I met Marilyn, my wife-to-be, midway in college, and she managed to at least get me to try occasionally.

During my first year, the freshman team played only three games, spending most of our time working as the dummy squad for the varsity. Naturally, this situation caused some unpleasant moments. One hot September afternoon a few days before a big game, everyone was a little uptight, causing tempers to flare. I was playing defensive back covering Earl McCullough. He ran a hook pattern at about fifteen yards, and I broke in front of him and knocked the ball down. I really felt like a hero until I heard Coach McKay's voice screaming at me, "You little son-of-a-bitch . . . we're trying to get ready for a big game, and you're out here fucking up our practice. You'll never play a minute for this team, you pissant. Now get the hell out of my sight and don't come back!" Needless to say, my forced march to the locker room was an eternity for me.

I put my gear in my locker, went to the dorm to pack, loaded my stuff in my car, and was about to head for home when Craig Fertig, an assistant coach, came running up and said, "Hold it, Bob. Coach sent me over to tell you how sorry he was for losing his temper. He didn't mean a thing he said 'cause he knows you're going to be a great one." He helped me unload my car and told me to go out and have dinner at Julies and just forget the whole incident. I fell for this, hook, line, and sinker, only because I wanted to. Good old Fertig. To this day, I suspect that

McKay had nothing to do with that apology. It probably never crossed the coach's mind that I was even upset.

John McKay was an intelligent, sharp-witted motivator who always stayed one step ahead of possible conflicts. For instance, in 1969, when everybody was growing long hair and mustaches against most coaches' wishes, McKay told the team, "You black guys have a thing about mustaches. It's apparently in your heritage. But you white guys, remember, it's not in *your* heritage, so forget it!" And that was that.

He was never close to his players. He did most of his coaching through his assistants from a tower or a golf cart on Bovard Field. This is where he affectionately received the name of "Lawrence Of Bovard." I had a lot of respect for John McKay. I only wish I could have known him better.

Things changed the next year. In the third game of my sophomore year, our wide receiver, Jimmy Lawrence, broke his collarbone. When I watched the John McKay show (which gave USC's coach the opportunity to whet the Trojan fans' appetite) on television the following week, I nearly fell off my chair when McKay stated, "He doesn't know it yet, but Bob Chandler is going to be the starting flanker against Cal this Saturday." Immediately I went out in the backyard and started to try to catch some passes.

I started the game, caught eight passes, one for a touchdown, gained 115 yards, and received a standing ovation from the crowd in the Coliseum. At long last, USC's sleeper had awakened, and the stardom that I had secretly hoped for was thrust upon me.

What I learned from all this at such a young age was that an athlete can never plan ahead. There are just too many variables that cannot be controlled. This unpredictability can have a major effect on one's life. Most ballplayers will deny the fact that everyone is just waiting for the next guy to get injured, but in the game of football, it's inevitable that one man's injury becomes the next guy's chance of a lifetime. I'll never forget in Oakland when Dan Pastorini broke his leg on the field, and the crowd literally cheered because they wanted Jim Plunkett to play. I had to convince myself they were cheering the situation, not the injury—I hoped. In a sense, civilized man hasn't progressed very far from the days of the Roman gladiators in the Circus Maximus.

The most tragic consequence of all is that football players—whether in high school, college or the pros—are motivated to continue playing after they've been injured. They keep telling themselves—as I did—that the injury is not that serious, and yet, in their collective hearts, they know that their athletic career is being pared away. They convince themselves they're okay and willing to continue no matter what the cost. By doing this, they slowly lose respect for their own well-being. They break down their natural barriers of self-preservation. That play-at-all-costs attitude has started and will continue until the body can no longer answer the bell. Think about it. Every day in the sports pages, you read about some great new player and you wonder where this guy came from. Five times out of ten, he never would've been playing unless some other teammate had gotten injured.

After my sophomore season, we had a big spring game. Jimmy Jones, a quarterback from Pennsylvania, had just transferred to USC, and he was throwing me everything. I caught—if you can believe this—fifteen passes, including five for touchdowns, and gained about 400 yards. The next day in the *Los Angeles Times,* I was picked as a dark horse for the Heisman trophy! Suddenly, it was me—the guy who our coach once said looked like a choir-boy—who was getting picked for all the preseason All-American teams. It was at that point, for the first time, that I started thinking seriously about the NFL. My dual personality took hold permanently. I could be superman on the football field, showing how tough I was and how much pain I could take. Simultaneously, I felt it was extremely important to be humble and modest in my everyday life. I wanted the public to be awed by me, on the one hand, and also to realize, on the other hand, that I was your basic, ordinary guy who had other talents and interests off the field.

My junior year, we played Northwestern in our opening game. I went down to catch a low ball, and the halfback speared me in my lower back. I wasn't sure what was damaged, but I couldn't feel my right leg, which scared the hell out of me. I hobbled off the field. Later, back at my apartment, I was in such agony that by the middle of the night, my roommate Gerry Mullins literally had to pick me up, carry me to his car, and take me to a hospital. After a battery of x-rays, John McKay came in and said matter-of-factly, "Looks like you broke your back." That was the good news. The bad news was that I would have to wear a body cast for six months. McKay told me not to worry, since he would try to get my year's eligibility back.

Later, after more tests, the doctors revised the earlier diagnosis. They decided that I was born with a crack in one vertebra, and the blow I sustained in the game had merely broken off four transverse processes from the spine. I was assured that I didn't need those little bones, but what they were really saying was that there was no way to replace those little bones. Having aggravated the birth defect, I suffered some nerve damage, which caused everyday movements like reaching for the telephone to feel like someone had stuck a hot poker in my spine.

I was fitted for a fiberglass brace to go around my back. Naturally, I was a little upset at having to miss the following week's game, but that was better than the whole season. I begged the team doctor to let me play in the third game of the season. Dr. Labriola, our orthopedic surgeon, said nothing, stared at me for a moment, and then asked me to bend over. After giving me a quick chop to my injured low back, he watched me fall down on one knee. While I was gasping for breath, he walked away muttering, "I don't think you're quite ready yet."

While watching that third game from the bench, I was just grateful that the guy who'd replaced me hadn't had enough time to do a great job. Since watching games tends to get a bit boring, I began staring at the cheerleaders and picked out the one with the best legs. That night I got her name and arranged for a mutual acquaintance to fix us up on a blind date two weeks later.

The following Saturday, I was back on the field wearing a

plaster brace, which made running very uncomfortable. I was at about 60 percent of my normal abilities, but once you're out on that field, you delude yourself into believing that you're playing great and can't get hurt again. My number had come up a few weeks ago and my back got smashed; by the luck of the draw, my number wasn't due to come up again for a long time—or so I told myself.

The first game back happened to be against Notre Dame back in South Bend. Notre Dame and USC were two of the top-ranked teams in the country, and this game was obviously a big one. In the fourth quarter, we were punting, and I was in at blocking back. Why, I have no idea—but that's where I was . . . me and my back brace. Lined up in the gap over me was Mike McCoy, a 295-pound defensive tackle. He ran over me like a Mack truck. I'm not sure I even slowed him down. The ball and McCoy came together about six inches off the punter's foot. The blocked punt resulted in a touchdown for Notre Dame and gave them a tie. I felt absolutely miserable, but what the hell . . . life must go on.

The next game was against Georgia Tech, and I was still forced to wear my brace. But none of this was preying on my mind because, as I mentioned, after the game was my first date with that cheerleader with the incredible legs. During the first quarter, I went sliding across the middle reaching out for a ball and collided with a defensive back, who grabbed my left hand and bent it back in the other direction. He did a superb job, since he broke three of my fingers, one knuckle, and cracked two bones up in the hand itself. Our trainer, Gary Tuthill, wrapped up my hand, and I went back out to finish the game. After all, Tommy Trojan would have done the same! Afterward, I went to the hospital where they put a plaster cast on my arm all the way up to my elbow.

I was forty-five minutes late for my date. That blind date was Marilyn Richardson, who later became my wife. The poor girl had no idea what she was getting into. Nevertheless, we had a good time that night despite my back brace, my hand and arm cast, and me deciding to get drunk because I was feeling sorry for myself.

Happily, my number did *not* come up again, and consequently I had no more serious injuries that season. Every Saturday morning, Tuthill and Jack Ward would take my hand out of the cast and wrap it as well as possible in order to play, and every Saturday night, they would put the cast back on. Needless to say, it took a helluva long time for the bones to knit, and to this day, my left hand has never regained its original strength. I wasn't surprised when my name didn't show up on any of the All-American teams that year; I was just lucky to have been able to play as much of the season as I did.

The highlight of that season—besides getting together with Marilyn—was the Trojans getting a bid to the Rose Bowl, where we would face Michigan. Being healthy for the first time that year, I was glad to be able to contribute to this big game. Contributed enough, in fact, to be awarded the MVP. Actually, it was awarded to me by default, since I wasn't that fantastic—it was just that nobody else did very much that day. We won the game, 10–3, and I scored the winning touchdown. That award was the brightest spot in my life at the time, and I remember hiding it in my locker after the game just in case the judges changed their minds and wanted it back.

By my senior year, Marilyn and I had an understanding that we planned to get married. Her father's a doctor, and he had hoped that his daughter would either marry a doctor or go to medical school herself. When she told her parents that she wanted them to meet her boyfriend, who was a wide receiver, they weren't too happy. Ultimately, both families gave us their blessings, and since Marilyn was one year behind me at college, we thought we might get married once she graduated.

Besides giving me some stability, Marilyn also encouraged me to concentrate a bit on my studies. During the first months of dating, we would study together in the basement of her sorority house, and she realized that I had the attention span of a gnat when it came to reading. However, her perseverance paid off in my doing relatively well, even though her grades took a nosedive that semester. But there were other compensations. She did get to see every movie that came out that year.

Despite some recurring lower-back pain, I managed to stay injury-free during my last season as a Trojan. We had a lousy record that year—six wins and four losses, which was unheard of at USC. Fourteen guys on our team were eventually drafted into professional football, and we still couldn't win. Since I had been elected captain of the team, I was called in for a meeting with Coach McKay, who wondered why such a talented squad had so many losses. We never really came up with a reason—other than times were a-changing. The country was at war in Vietnam. The campuses were protesting. The students—including the athletes—were questioning things. And for the first time, football was not the big thing on campus that it used to be.

I did dislocate a couple of fingers that year and was knocked out once or twice. Whenever a player becomes unconscious on the field, it always seems strange to hear the doctors and trainers say, "He's okay, it was just his head." Having been knocked out six or seven times in my career to date, the hardest thing is going back to the bench and trying to remember the plays that you've committed to memory before the game. The harder you try, the longer it takes. So the experienced knockout-ees just sit back and let it happen.

After the season, I was one of three from our team selected to play in the East-West Shrine Game, and I couldn't wait, since this would be a terrific opportunity to impress the pro football scouts. Fortunately, a school like USC is the closest thing you can get to a training camp for the pros. We had all gotten used to big pressure, huge crowds, big buildups and terrible letdowns—everything the pros had to offer. We went up to Palo Alto to practice for a week before the game, which was held at Stanford. I felt like a little kid in a candy store because I was surrounded by so many players I had heard so much about.

After the first practice a ball boy came up to me, introduced himself, and told me that someday he was going to be a pro ballplayer. I said, "Sure, kid, sounds great!" His name was Dan Fouts.

I got to start, which made me feel like I really belonged. My team, the West, won. I caught a few passes and played pretty well overall—so I was satisfied I could play with the big boys. Now it was just sit back and wait for the good old draft.

By the early spring, I had convinced myself that I would be a top draft choice. I'd been USC's leading receiver for three years and was captain of what was considered one of the country's best teams. If any of the scouts had questions about my size, my speed, or my injuries, I figured those points could be argued, and besides, I showed them in my senior year that I could stay relatively healthy.

Despite my optimism about playing professionally, I must've had some nagging doubts because I took the law school entrance exam, and I scored fairly well. At least I had that and my bachelor's degree as a backup in case things didn't work out the way I wanted. Marilyn was very supportive of my football ambitions, but I don't think she ever thought I would really make it and end up spending over a decade in the sport. She had decided to get her master's degree in education and continue with her own ambitions, regardless of my eventual fate.

During my last couple of years at USC, while working at a summer job at the recreation department in Culver City, I met and became good friends with one of the finest receivers I would ever come across in my lifetime: Billy Parks. Billy was going to Long Beach State at the time, and both of us were anticipating a shot at a pro career.

Billy was subconsciously everything I wanted to be. I know that sounds strange since I was the big shot at USC, and Billy was a relative unknown at L.B. State. But this man was a free spirit. He was intelligent, aware, and very politically minded. He didn't read Knute Rockne—he read Bertrand Russell. He was an atypical football player who just happened to catch a football as well as any man alive.

Billy Parks went on to play several years of pro football, and he had his moments of brilliance on the field. But he never lasted because he questioned things. He asked "Why?" too many times. As a player, you just play, and you can't concern yourself too much with the idiocy that surrounds so much of the game.

Playing for the Cowboys, Billy's downfall came before a game one season in Dallas. It was raining like hell that particular day when Parks entered the field for pregame warm-ups. He looked up and noticed that with the opening at the top of the Texas Stadium dome, it only rained on the players. He suddenly felt as though he were in a bottle and the whole world was watching him. He just got pissed off realizing that the big fat cats with their cowboy hats and long cigars could sit in the front row of the stadium and remain completely dry.

When Billy looked down at the field and saw that there was about two inches of water on it, he said that the only thing he had ever done in two inches of water was to go sliding on a slip and slide. And that's precisely what he did! He lined up at one end of Texas Stadium, ran like hell, and slid on his stomach. Needless to say, Billy was not cut out of the Dallas Cowboy mold. He eventually left football and moved to Hawaii where he now makes furniture almost as well as he caught a football.

In the early weeks of April, you could almost taste the tension of waiting for the pro draft at USC. Many of my close friends were on the team, and we placed bets on who would go where. I was hoping that I'd be picked by a west coast team. Don't all receivers want to play in the sun? Some of the professional teams had sent out questionnaires to potential draftees. I wish I'd saved the one from one of the teams because it was unbelievable. A typical question might be something like, "If you were walking across the street and saw a dying bird in the gutter, would you pick it up or step on it?" Since they were looking for real competitors, they structured the test to measure one's competitiveness and aggressiveness. I guess the test was supposed to identify the guys with that killer attitude. I figured I had failed that test because I would have picked the bird up and tried to nurse it back to health—a really sensitive person, I guess.

On the first day of the draft, a bunch of us gathered at an apartment to wait for the fateful phone calls. The system is pretty simple in that they do it all in New York City, and before each choice is announced, they call the man to tell him where he might be in August. The first of seven rounds started at 8:30 A.M., and it was Pittsburgh in the third round asking for my roommate, Gerry Mullins, telling him they were going to draft him next. I was truly happy for Gerry, particularly since it was worth some good money for him because the first three rounds contained fairly large salaries and bonuses. After that, we all started playing cards, and my heart was beginning to pound because that damn phone wasn't ringing. The time ticked by slower than I wished to remember, and soon we were watching the news on television. The announcer came on and said that the San Francisco Forty-Niners had just taken a receiver from USC in the third round. I let out a huge sigh of relief, thinking how great it would be to be based in San Francisco. But I also thought it odd that they didn't phone me first. Then the announcer said the receiver was Sam Dickerson. Holy shit, was I embarrassed. Sam was a good receiver, but it was obvious, at least to me, that he just wasn't as good as I was. This day was turning into a real humiliating experience for me.

I was getting so uneasy and embarrassed that I left and went back to my parents' home in Whittier. I sat like a hound dog in front of the TV set, and my interest was piqued when they announced in the fifth round that another wide receiver was taken by Detroit. I rationalized to myself that it wasn't totally bad being chosen in the fifth round, and as for Detroit, well, I could learn to live there and like it. The player was Herman Franklin. Oh, God, what a day this had become. Franklin, who was second string, never played an offensive down at USC; however, he had tied the world record in the high hurdles. What horrible logic! They probably thought Herman could become another Earl McCullough, who had graduated from USC two years earlier. He was potentially a good player, and obviously unproven, yet they drafted him on his speed alone. McCullough became Rookie of the Year with Detroit, but he didn't last in the pros very long because you just can't do it on speed alone. Without a solid foundation, based on sound techniques, it's hard to last very long.

By this time, I actually felt too embarrassed to face Marilyn, let alone my parents. As for my teammates, I assumed that I'd complete my last few months wearing a paper bag over my head. Maybe I'd call myself "The Unknown Player." By 9 P.M., when the phone rang, I was contemplating a permanent move to the Fiji Islands. It was O. J. Simpson, whom I knew from the two years he played for USC. O. J. said, "Buffalo just drafted you in the seventh round!"

I couldn't understand any of this, since it was a good four hours after the draft ended. I asked, "Why are *you* calling me?"

"Because," said O. J., "I run things around here, and I told them to draft you."

I was bewildered but it didn't matter. In fact, nothing else mattered at that moment. I thanked O. J. for calling, and almost as an afterthought, I asked him where Buffalo was. I knew it was in New York State, but I didn't have any idea where.

A postscript to this demoralizing day is that I never did get a call from Buffalo. The next day I read all about it in the *LA Times*. Not only was Buffalo a lousy team, but I was also facing the very real possibility of not even making it, since their first pick was J. D. Hill, a receiver from Arizona State. Besides, they already had two great receivers in Haven Moses and Marlin Briscoe, which made me realize how short my stay in Buffalo might be.

I decided to use O. J.'s agent, Chuck Barnes, to help me negotiate my contract, though I knew full well that Buffalo would tell me to take a hike if I asked for too much. I signed a three-year contract, and they gave me a $3,500 signing bonus and an annual salary starting at $15,000 the first year, $17,500 the second, and $20,000 the third. I don't want to come off sounding like an ungrateful bastard, because at the time that was big money for a guy like me. What really upset me was thinking that a first-round choice like J. D. Hill probably got a $200,000 bonus on top of a big salary. No one ever said the world was just, but this, at least to me, was a little ridiculous.

Shortly after the football draft, my buddies and I were assembled again around the television set. This time we were watching the military draft lottery, and unlike the NFL draft, my birth date was the second one picked. Mind you, this was in 1971, and thousands of guys were being sent regularly to Vietnam. I contacted the Buffalo Bills after I received my induction papers and notice to appear for my physical. Cheerily, they told me that if I passed the physical, they would fly me back there and use some connections to get me into a reserve unit in New York. I could then do my weekends for six years during the off-season. This was just another example of how football players are taken care of and protected, at least until they get out on the field.

I phoned Dr. Labriola, the team doctor at USC, and asked him to write a letter about my back and gather my x-rays from the hospital. He agreed that I had a legitimate problem and would comply. He then said he'd heard about my decision to play pro football. Trying not to alarm me, the doctor told me that if I received the right kind of blow to my weakened vertebra, I would end up as a paraplegic. That was just the kind of news I needed as I was getting ready for Buffalo's training camp that coming summer.

My army physical was exactly like what I had seen in the movies. Hundreds of naked guys covered with goose bumps were waiting to go from station to station for various examinations. I had passed every station so far with honors, and was sitting on a bench with four other guys outside the last station—the orthopedic exam. As I waited, I saw two guys walk out of the station, and they were crying. One was shaking his head, mumbling something like, "How could they take me?"

When my turn came, I told the doctor about my back problem and gave him the letter and the x-rays. After taking what seemed like an hour to read the material (and he was even moving his lips as he read), he excused himself, saying that he had to consult with another doctor. Meanwhile, I was sweating and hoping that Buffalo wasn't kidding about that reserve unit.

The army doctor came back and said, "How're you going to like jumping out of airplanes and crawling through ditches?"

A cold sweat broke out on my forehead, but I decided that I wasn't going to make a fool of myself and break down like the guys I saw earlier. So, matter-of-factly, I said, "I'll get used to it."

"Too bad," he replied, "you failed, so get the hell out of here." He seemed very angry because he knew who I was. As I walked out, he said, "By the way, I hope your pro career goes well."

There was a bit of justice in this wacky world. The army didn't want to be saddled with a back problem—yet, for all intents and purposes, I was physically strong enough to play professional football, I hoped!

3

Getting the Bends in Buffalo—The Rookie Year

Rain has hastened night
Windows are a blur
Changing faces
With
each
drop;

Gaining a certain charm
That vanishes
With the clouds—

As the sun creeps through the
darkness,
the character is lost.

The windows become
expressionless
and easily seen through!

—BOB CHANDLER
1973—South Exit 56 Motel
Buffalo, New York

Shortly before I graduated from USC, we had what the pro teams called a minicamp romp in Buffalo that was guaranteed to imbue each newcomer with a lethal case of paranoia.

You could cut the humidity with a knife the day I flew into Buffalo and checked into a dubious-looking hotel in downtown Buffalo. When I inquired at the desk how much the room was, a lady with a red wig and false eyelashes winked and replied, "How much do you want to spend, sweetheart?"

At this minicamp, all of the rookies got to meet the various members of the coaching staff and trainers, and we went through orientation meetings and workouts twelve hours a day. I didn't have much time to get a feel for the city. But I did notice there was a bar on every corner and they stayed open till 4:00 A.M.

Although all of the rookies were outwardly friendly to one another, it seemed that deep down each guy was studying everyone else and comparing how he measured up to other guys at his position, and especially the top draft choices. I'll never forget meeting Dennis Shaw, the quarterback of the Bills who had been chosen the AFC Rookie of the Year in 1970. With a big grin, he said, "Boy, I'm glad you're here. Now I've got someone to throw to who can catch the ball." I thought he was kidding, since the Bills already had such gifted receivers as Haven Moses and Marlin Briscoe.

Graduating from USC was a big thrill for me and an even bigger one for my parents. Afterward, those first two months of summer gave me a chance to lead a totally physical existence—lifting weights, running and catching the ball. I bounced back from the combined nightmares of the football and military drafts and was feeling very grateful for the chance to go play professional football. I was getting excited about the prospect of paying my dues in Buffalo.

The downside of that summer was working out how to handle the six-month separation from Marilyn—that is, if I made the team. I was sorry that my absence would make her senior year sort of anticlimactic, but there was really nothing we could do. But she was as willing to sacrifice her good times as I was. Even though it didn't seem fair for me to go off and experience a new city, new people, and a new life while she had to stay at college, I was actually glad to be going off alone and looking forward to the challenge. Maybe, if I played my cards wrong, I'd be back in Los Angeles sooner than I hoped.

Because your rookie year in professional football is mined with so many bombs that can destroy your career in a hurry, I decided to move to Buffalo with as few belongings as possible—just in case. I didn't even want to drive my car there because the idea of having to drive it back alone after being cut by the team was too painful to even think about. As a seventh-round draft choice, I wasn't too eager to show up at camp with my car and a U-Haul filled with all my belongings. That's like saying, "Here I am, guys. I've decided to stay ten years or so."

I agreed to drive east with a former USC buddy, Sandy Durko, who was heading to Cincinnati as a second-year defensive back for the Bengals. Sandy was driving his Corvette to Ohio, so I decided to go along for the ride. I thought I would work out a couple of days in Cincinnati, then just fly from Cincinnati to Buffalo. My day of departure was a tough one. Marilyn had spent the night with me at my apartment in Manhattan Beach. We got up, had breakfast, made some mutual promises, and before I knew it, she was standing there waving goodbye to me as I drove off with a lump in my throat. Despite the many times I told her how I'd miss her, these words seemed very hollow as we drove down Highland Avenue in this shiny new sports car ready to conquer new worlds.

About two hours outside of Los Angeles, we started getting carried away with our freedom and decided to detour to Las Vegas. After all, it didn't seem that far out of the way. We nearly collapsed in Vegas from heat exhaustion when we tried to work out in 110-degree weather. So, after a big night on the town, we packed up and hit the highway the next morning. Another highlight of this "playboys'" tour of the country was stopping in Oklahoma City on a weekend. Going into a bar, we asked the pretty bartendress what there was to do in Oklahoma City on a Saturday night. "Well," she drawled, "you picked a bad night."

By the time we arrived in Cincinnati, three days later, I was getting anxious to get to Buffalo and get started with training camp as quickly as possible.

The official site for the Buffalo Bills' training camp was Niagara University, which reminded me of a typical eastern university with its giant elms and ivy-covered walls. Coming from Los Angeles it was a very pleasant, serene setting on the banks of Niagara Falls. Ironically, I didn't know at the time that amidst all this beauty, we were training right on top of the Love Canal. I don't even want to think about all the water I drank and showered in that may have been contaminated.

My biggest worry during training camp was just in making the team. I was determined, and kept telling myself what a good receiver I was to preclude my becoming infected with the mass fear of being cut. I shared a dormitory room with Greg Jones, a second-year running back from UCLA, who eventually became a very close friend, but whenever I'd start complaining about something, he'd always shoot back, "You think that's lousy, well, listen to this . . ." which was the common response of all players.

As a rookie coming from the warm womb of being a living legend at college, I needed someone to whom I could tell my troubles as well as someone who'd give me some positive strokes. But players didn't relate to each other in that way now that we had become professionals. It seemed as if no one wanted to get very close to another player for the simple reason that the guy you befriended may be cut or traded at any time. It was the same peculiar logic that affects soldiers about to go into battle. You know, the guys who ignore their buddies because they realize that they may lose them.

The method that the Buffalo Bills used to cut players was frightening in itself. It was so efficient and at the same time terrifying that it seemed to have been devised by either an ex-CIA agent or a Mafia hit-man. At night the coaching staff would assemble privately to discuss what had taken place so far in camp and on that day in particular. It was at these meetings that they made the decisions on the next day's roster cuts. I don't know what criteria they were using, but in these sessions, a lot of guys had their careers altered and consequently their lives changed permanently. The next morning, a staff "bearer of sad tidings" would knock on the cut player's door at 7:00 A.M. to tell him the coach wanted to see him, and "bring your playbook." Within the hour, the player would have his bag packed and be whisked off to the airport to catch the next plane to his hometown. All of a sudden, this player with whom you'd worked and sweated on the practice fields had become a nonperson and was gone. His locker had been emptied, and in a few weeks not many players even remembered his name. It seemed uncivilized to me not to let the deposed player have a few extra hours to say goodbye to whomever and maybe even have a last lunch with the guys. However, in retrospect, it was probably the most merciful way to do the deed. The cut player was too humiliated to face his peers and start telling them about the uncertainty of his future and perhaps his money problems.

During my rookie year, I remember seeing one player, whom I hardly knew, walking rapidly through the Niagara campus with tears streaming down his face, as he was carrying his playbook to the coach's office. As he walked by I could feel his frustration and disappointment of having failed. But in actuality it wasn't really failing, it was the slipping away of a dream. Reality had slapped him in the face. Now it was time to join the real world.

Early in training camp, I felt extremely lucky because John Rauch, the Bills' head coach, told me that I was the closest guy in the game to becoming another Fred Biletnikoff. My head swelled only for twenty-four hours, because the next day Rauch quit!

The next week I pulled a hamstring muscle and strained my groin, but I kept playing because rookies couldn't afford to take even an hour off as long as the "Turk," the man who bore news of the cuts, was still roaming the halls at dawn. Whenever I phoned my parents or Marilyn, I'd give them the mixed reviews of The Bob Chandler Story—that I was doing well on the field but didn't know what would happen at 7:00 A.M. the following morning.

When final cutdown day came and went without anyone asking me to turn in my playbook, I experienced feelings of relief that were indescribable. I wanted to celebrate, but since I hadn't gotten close to anyone at camp, I had no one with whom to go out and get drunk.

The Bills' owner, Ralph Wilson, had appointed Harvey Johnson as interim head coach when Rauch had quit in a dispute with management. Harvey had built his reputation as a tremendous scout, but even he would be quick to admit that he was not head coach material. As the season progressed, Harvey would sit silently watching the films of the previous week's game. It was as if he was watching portents of his own doom and could do nothing about it. Meanwhile, every one of the assistant coaches was devising his own strategy to take over the reins when Harvey received his walking papers.

Having survived training camp cuts, I was at least optimistic about completing my rookie year. I was feeling so good that I went out and bought a 1953 Chevy for just under a hundred dollars; it had no heater and a radio that played only when it was in the mood, but it fit my low-profile rookie life-style.

As far as soaking up the glamour of pro football was concerned, I was underwhelmed by War Memorial Stadium, where the Bills were still playing in 1971. It looked like a deteriorating B-movie set compared with the Los Angeles Coliseum where I'd spent the past four years. If the stadium was painful (particularly since there was never enough hot water for the rookies, who always showered last), then our practice field, with the unlikely name of Amherst Recreation Center, was downright laughable. Picture, if you can, a playing field adjoining an ice rink and parking lot with two trailers—one of which was used for the offense meetings and the other for the defense. The humor came in how we utilized this facility particularly when the weather was bad. Once all of the rookies were given special commando boots and were asked to go out on the field to pack down the snow. Whenever there was freezing rain, we had to run our drills in the parking lot, tripping over the concrete parking dividers. Sometimes when the weather was unspeakable, we even practiced in the ice rink and its surrounding corridors, where we had to keep from running into Coke and candy machines.

I found a room in a downtown apartment-hotel because I really wanted to immerse myself in the city. I felt it was important for me to see how the people of Buffalo lived instead of isolating myself with football players. By patronizing the bars and restaurants of downtown Buffalo, I really got to understand the love-hate feelings that the fans had toward the Bills. I realized it was a tempestuous relationship when O. J. Simpson warned me before my first game to keep my helmet on when walking on and off the field and never to walk next to the coach. At the stadium, the fans sat about eight feet from the players, with only a short unstable picket fence to separate them. After losing our first game, I was jogging off the field and something hit my leg with a thud. I looked down and found, to my disbelief, that someone had gotten so upset they took their false teeth out and threw them at us. Passions ran very deep in this city.

The Bills had been doing poorly for the past few years, and the fans in this sports-minded metropolis acted like rejected lovers. After all, Buffalo had replaced Philadelphia as the butt of most jokes about dismal cities, and a place with a metropolitan-sized inferiority complex needed a winning football team to regain its respectability. It took a few years. I understood that through sports the people of Buffalo could show the people of LA or Dallas that their city was just as good. Their football team was an extension of their city.

I can safely say that I started my pro career in the sub-basement, since the Bills won one and lost thirteen games that season. Since our fans abused us with epithets and flying objects during our seven home games, it soon became refreshing, and a helluva lot safer, to play in other cities. These towns welcomed us with open arms, since playing the Buffalo Bills seemed to guarantee another notch on their teams' winning records. Although most of the players kept pretty much to themselves after practice and games in Buffalo, it was just the opposite when we went on the road. On out-of-town trips we were shepherded around like a bunch of convent girls. Some man of infinite wisdom years ago came up with the notion that football players are not capable of functioning on their own when the team is traveling.

On a short hop, we'd fly in the day before the game, and when we flew to the west coast, we'd arrive two days before the game. On west coast trips, the time change was always a problem. Teams never really knew how to deal with it. Sometimes, we would leave two days before the game. Other times, we'd depart just one day prior to playing. And once, we even kept our watches on Buffalo time. This proved to be very tough on us. I mean, you're conditioned to go to bed when Johnny Carson's clowning around—not to *Hee Haw* at 7:30 P.M.! Believe it or not, they did this and even woke us up at 5:00 A.M. on game day. Naturally, we got beaten badly that day. We'd all stay at the same hotel, and it was usually two guys to a room unless you were a veteran who'd been on the team a long time. Having to assemble for pregame meals wasn't too bad except that you were always looking at your watch to be there on time. The worst part was the nightly security check, when the coaches and a hotel security guard would check each room, shining a flashlight on the beds to make sure we were in after curfew. I would generally turn in early on the night before the game, and after sleeping soundly for an hour, I'd be awakened at 11:00 P.M. by some considerate souls who were verifying the fact that I was sleeping. After that, it would often take hours before I could get back to sleep.

The day of the game was a different matter entirely. Psyching yourself up for the game now became your major concern. Players psych up in many different ways. Some don't talk, while others never stop talking. Some guys listen to music, or sleep, or get violent. A few guys throw up. You can bet that one or more of these techniques are used in every NFL locker room throughout the country on Sunday mornings. A couple of hours before the game, I would find a quiet corner in the locker room, make a comfortable bed out of clean towels, lie down on the towels while holding a football as my security blanket and visualize the entire game in my mind—from the first play to the final gun. My imagination usually surpassed my performance.

Mark Van Egan, a great fullback for the Raiders, never felt he was ready until he threw up repeatedly. Raymond Chester, an All-Pro tight end, would engulf himself in music for two hours before the game. Dave Casper was the greatest, though. He had a nonchalant act where he would pretend he didn't care about anything. He'd sing, dance, joke around, or sleep. I believed that inside he must have been churning because nobody could have been that good on the field and that relaxed beforehand.

Shortly after the season began, Busty Underwood, my new roommate, a rookie quarterback from Texas Christian University, and I were walking off the practice field, and we were stopped by Dennis Shaw, the quarterback who had praised me at rookie camp. Dennis said he wanted to invite us to a good home-cooked meal at his townhouse that night. We arrived exactly on time at seven, and Dennis introduced us to his wife, a very nice lady who had gone to the trouble of cooking an elaborate meal. They poured us glasses of wine, and we sat around talking for five minutes or so. All of a sudden, Dennis just stood up and, without a word, walked upstairs and went to bed. His wife told Busty and me to come to the table, and we sat down to a great dinner. Since she never said a word about where Dennis had gone, we never mentioned it either, but the conversation throughout the meal was terribly strained, as all of us felt very uncomfortable. We left right after dinner, and subsequently Dennis never said anything about the night. He also must've heard that we were terrible company because he never invited us over again.

Dennis Shaw was playing fairly well that season, but he was having a bad year emotionally. He would have fits of frustration, lose his temper, and then sulk for a long time. From the way he acted, I was learning why pro ballplayers should learn to keep their emotions deep inside them while playing. In our fifth game, which was played at home, Dennis seemed to be more on edge than usual during the second quarter. Every time one of our plays failed, Dennis would take it personally. Besides the fact that we were getting beat up pretty good, Dennis appeared to be distracted by the hoots and jeers of the fans.

Gradually, a group of little black kids stationed themselves about ten feet behind our bench and started chanting every swear word in the language against Dennis. I was sitting next to O.J., and as we were talking, I could hear simultaneously the verbal abuse these kids were heaping on Dennis. All of a sudden, Dennis turned around and screamed, "Why don't you shut the hell up, you fucking little niggers!" As I slouched as far down on the bench as I could without falling over, needless to say, the shit hit the fan. Marlin Briscoe refused to go back into the game as long as Dennis was still playing. I had to jump in and take Marlin's place, even though I hadn't warmed up or played at all that day.

At half time, after word of the incident had spread in the locker room, Al Cowlings, Haven Moses, and the rest of the black players on our team stated flatly that they would not play in the same game with Dennis Shaw. Then Dennis stood up and made a futile effort to explain himself, but unfortunately he just dug himself deeper into the hole. I felt humiliated for him and at the same time I was just embarrassed for being a white guy in the middle of such idiotic racism, whether intended or not. I may have been naive, but I never saw any overt black-versus-white antagonism while I was at USC, and the scene that occurred that day made me want to jump into my locker and hide.

Finally, O.J. got into the fray and was persuasive enough to calm down most of the black players by letting Dennis know what an asshole he was. But Dennis had crossed an invisible line, and hell could freeze over before he could regain what he had lost that day. The team quieted down, and we went back on the field to lose the game. No one spoke to Dennis on the bench or in the game, and it seemed to mark the beginning of the slow demise of Dennis Shaw. Never again was there any outward sign of hostility or indignation, but among the key players, a division had been drawn that became indelible. As it turned out, the following year Dennis was hurt a few times and therefore played sporadically, and it was during my third year that Dennis was eventually traded to St. Louis. Obviously, there was no big going-away party for the man.

The only good news about playing for Buffalo that season was the fact that we'd all be home for Christmas, since there wouldn't be any playoff games for the likes of us. Sliding along at the bottom of the American Conference was terribly demoralizing. During the final game against the Chiefs in Kansas City, I was determined to make a decent showing, if only to have something positive to carry me through the off-season.

O.J. had made reservations for both of us to catch a 5:30 P.M. plane for Los Angeles. When I told him how tight that would be, he laughed, saying we could always shower on the plane.

In the locker room before the game, I saw O.J. going up to each guy and talking to him. I thought to myself, "Isn't that something! A great player like Simpson was trying to fire up the guys before the last game of a disastrous season." I soon found out that he was jokingly telling everyone to stay in bounds, keep the ball on the ground, and get no penalties. That way, the clock would keep running and we'd make our 5:30 flight. So much for college pep talks! He wasn't really serious, I don't think!

Early in the second quarter, Kansas City was going to punt, and if the ball was kicked badly and short, my job as upback was to fair-catch it. However, if it was a good kick, the deep man would take it, and I was to pick out the most dangerous man or first man coming downfield and take him out.

The punt sailed over my head, so I started looking for the most dangerous man coming downfield. My first thought was: how could *he* be the first man downfield? He, of course, was good old number 97, Buck Buchanan, a 6-foot-9-inch, 295-pound defensive end. Then, it suddenly occurred to me that nobody was blocking because nobody wanted to get hurt and have to spend the off-season in Buffalo rehabilitating the injury. So, I went at him full speed and hit him in his softest spot—his stomach. The next thing I knew he had picked me up by my little Pop Warner shoulder pads, and as my feet were dangling in the air, he looked me straight in the eye and said, "The punt returner's already been tackled, asshole." I mumbled, "Thank you," and slunk off the field feeling grateful that I was spared the inconvenience of spending Christmas in a wheelchair. I'm sure the coaches never saw this incident because I was invited back for another year.

Needless to say, O.J. and I made our plane. He had booked our reservations in first class, in which I'd never flown. And because he was O.J., the airline people actually let us buy our tickets right on the airplane. Everywhere O.J. went, he was always the star of the show. Being completely unknown, I felt a little self-conscious around him, fearing that people would think I was just another big fan or merely a hanger-on.

As the flight progressed, the passengers were getting drunker and drunker in the first-class area, and before long, the word was out that O.J. was among them. As bad as the Bills had played that year, O.J. was still regarded as a separate entity; he could really rise above our stench and come out smelling like a rose. Before long, a parade of passengers came up to O.J. asking for autographs or just wanting to bullshit with him. Most of them would start by saying something like, "I hate to bother you, O.J. . . ." and O.J. would look up with a mock angry expression and kiddingly reply, "So . . . don't!" Most people never expected that kind of answer, so consequently they would either never hear it or ignore it altogether. If somebody did hear it, a blank expression would come over their face until Simpson would flash that big, familiar smile and say, "Just kidding." It was remarkable how O.J. would handle everybody amiably and with incredible poise.

I was vicariously pretending that I was a household name like O.J. Would I be able to handle celebrityhood as well as he? I began fantasizing that people would probably assume that what appeared to be shyness really meant that I was conceited and didn't want to be bothered. As much as they're idolized by the public, professional football players are often rudely reminded that they wouldn't be where they are if it weren't for the millions of people who ultimately pay the players' salaries. Laughing aloud, I caused my daydream to disappear. Here, I had just completed my rookie year, was still virtually unknown, got to play a little for a poorly coached team that had reached a new depth in the NFL, was receiving one of the smallest salaries in modern-day pro football, and while I was sitting next to a celebrated football hero, I was pretending to be rich and famous too. Yes, I was certainly getting carried away with myself, but I was just beginning to realize that those kinds of fantasies were what kept me coming back year after year for more punishment.

4

Bloodied But Unbowed in Buffalo—The Early Years

Remember, when we're worlds apart,
And when you've taken half my heart,
That no two ever were as we
And no two e'er again will be.

At nighttime, when the mist is deep,
And you are drifting into sleep,
Somewhere, someone thinks of you
And all the things that you will do.

With time, by fate, our paths should cross,
You'll find me dwelling not on loss,
But on the moments we have shared
Through love that cannot be compared.

—MARILYN CHANDLER
1973—Whittier, California

With my rookie year snugly under my belt and the fact that I survived physically intact, I was really looking forward to that first off-season. I was glad to be in Los Angeles where I could be in the sun reading my Christmas cards. It was great not having to face another day of trudging through the slushy snow of Buffalo. The best part, however, was being with Marilyn again.

I missed her a lot during those six months and grew to rely on our long-distance calls as a means of buoying my spirits whenever they sagged. She was that steady rock I so desperately needed. I called Marilyn every night. Sometimes, I'd go back and try calling three or four times an evening if I couldn't reach her. I still have vivid memories of freezing-cold phone booths where I would go to make my calls, trying to escape the guys or the noise of a bar to get some privacy.

Carrying on a serious relationship at twenty-two years of age is not an easy proposition. And trying to do it 3,500 miles apart is damn near impossible. Marilyn was lonely. She really couldn't date, since I didn't want her to—so it was a pretty empty six months. What a warped double standard I had. It was perfectly okay for me to go out, have a few beers, and enjoy meeting my female fans in Buffalo, but the thought of Marilyn doing something similar was hard to take. It was a rocky six months. I was spending all my time and energy trying to make it in pro football, while Marilyn was trying to understand what the future held for her. So, needless to say, our reunion was a real adjustment. Spending that first year in Buffalo was enough to make anybody get married. Thus, the date was set for June 10, and knowingly, we both climbed aboard the rollercoaster. If I was fortunate enough to continue playing professional football, how would we handle a six-month on-and-off-again marriage? It could never be the kind of union that Marilyn or any woman in her right mind would dream about.

By this time, Marilyn had decided to go into teaching, and she needed a year of graduate school to get her teaching credentials. She felt very strongly about having her own identity, and I agreed, because in this past year I had met a number of my teammates' wives. Most of these women seemed like appendages of their husbands, and although they thought they knew a great deal about football, I found spending time with a Flossie Fullback or Teresa Tackle to be very depressing.

Marilyn and I finally agreed to trying out the half-year-together and half-year-apart routine. At least for the upcoming year, it wouldn't be too taxing, since we'd be together until July, and shortly thereafter, she'd be working hard at getting her master's in education and busy student teaching.

After getting an apartment together in the Wilshire District of LA, Marilyn finished her last semester at USC while I ended up taking a class there just to keep my mind from atrophying. Our landlord worked at the Los Angeles Athletic Club, and he convinced me to take a part-time job there at the check-in desk. It was one of those sobering jobs (like waiting on tables) that everyone should do at one time in their lives. You can really get your values straightened out when you work in a menial position.

Although word got out that I was Bob Chandler from USC and now played in the NFL, it didn't impress too many people. I found that most of the wealthy business and professional men treated me like an invisible peasant. The members were supposed to place their valuables in a sack, hand the sack to me, then I'd place it in a drawer, while they took their own towels. Some of the members would just dump all of their stuff in front of me and then expect me to run after them with the towels. That, needless to say, didn't work out too well. Even though I got to work out in the club's elaborate gym after hours, I was still in a "tote dat barge, lift dem bales" mode, which taught me a lot about respecting the dignity of people who serve us everywhere.

On June 10, Marilyn and I were married. I had never been to Hawaii, so we decided to go there for our honeymoon, and it was absolutely magnificent. Every day, we enjoyed all the things that you see on the travel posters, and each evening, we'd run on the beach and then have an exotic drink while enjoying the spectacular sunset. The last few days of our wedding trip were fairly grim, since we both knew that I'd be heading back to Buffalo as soon as we returned to LA. We thought we had prepared ourselves, but this parting was much worse than the previous year. Although we were now married, Marilyn was apprehensive. I was shuffling off to Buffalo for six months of "bachelorhood." It was the kind of story that keeps marriage counselors in business.

I was off to year two in the Buffalo Bills training camp. I felt as if I were really on a roll. Being injury-free that first year convinced me that I was invulnerable and could damn near do anything. Also, I was one of the few people in this country who could honestly admit to liking what I did for a living. I had adjusted to a disgusting season using the worst facilities imaginable, and now I was about to go marching off to glory again. Not even the sneers and jeers at my laughable part-time job could deter my thinking I was something special.

Arriving back east in the first week of July, I learned the good news that we were no longer without a leader. Harvey Johnson wasn't fired; he merely resumed his former position as head scout, and I could almost hear his sigh of relief. Our new head coach was Lou Saban, who had just left Denver and was returning to the Bills for the second time as head coach.

Training camp was held again at Niagara University, and on that very first night when the entire team and staff had their first general meeting, I knew instinctively that things would never again be the same for the Buffalo Bills. After we had all assembled, Saban waited a few minutes before entering, as if he wanted to build our anticipation. It reminded me of the way the President always walks in last when addressing the House and Senate. Nobody was playing "Hail to the Chief" when Lou walked in, but it would have been appropriate. Appearances are deceiving because Lou looked more like a bookie than a coach. For a few minutes, he just stared at us with fierce-looking eyes. This unprepossessing man with his hair combed straight back, wearing a sweat shirt that was two sizes too big and baggy khaki pants, in black coaching shoes with crepe soles, and sporting tinted glasses, was the anointed one who was to bring respectability to the wayward Buffalo Bills.

After he had thoroughly intimidated all of us with his scowl, he proceeded to tell us that the party was over. He said that he had no use for players who would run the other way in the last game of the season to keep from getting hurt. I felt my face turning red remembering the getaway that O.J. and I had perpetrated last December. Saban claimed he had a three-year plan to turn the team around, and he was going to weed out any player who wasn't giving everything he had. He said he wanted to end up with forty-five players who would battle for sixty minutes and, win or lose, would start getting some damn respect.

For the first time in my professional career, I was witnessing a mature, systematic approach to the game that was worthy of the highest standards set by the NFL. This is what I had read about as a kid. What I liked most about Lou Saban was his consistency. He treated everyone the same and treated us all like men. He taught us to believe in ourselves. He had faith in the adage that to gain respect, you must give respect. First of all, he made sure that every guy had a private room in the dormitories at camp. Next, we had relatively short workouts on the field, because Lou didn't believe in working us until we dropped just to let us know who was boss. At our nightly meetings, after he covered the necessary material, we were dismissed. Some meetings lasted less than fifteen minutes. It was a far cry from the previous year when we were kept in meetings for over two hours simply because the coaches didn't want to give us all that free time to go out and have a few beers. Saban never sent any of the assistant coaches to the dorms to check on the 11:00 P.M. curfew, since he knew that the players who were trying to do well on the field had enough sense to get the proper amount of sleep. In sum, he made us all feel important and independent—we were men who could take care of our own business and ourselves.

The next big awakening I had at training camp came when Saban declared that all of the wide receivers had to block. He didn't care how well you caught the ball or what a great pattern runner you were. He said simply, "All that stuff is great, but our priority here is running the football. And to run the ball effectively the wide receivers must block."

The next day before practice, the receivers got new face masks in the form of a cage across the front, which was a little terrifying since most of us were used to wearing a single bar. Saban then gave us a drill to find out which guys were willing to play football his way. We lined up in our wide-receiver positions and were facing linebackers who tipped the scales at an average weight of 225 pounds. Saban would then blow his whistle, and we would turn and come down on these linebackers in an attempt at a crack-back block. I was scared shitless, but I figured I had no choice, since this was the profession I wanted to pursue for the next few years. Our linebackers were delighted to see these skinny little WR's coming at them full speed. After all, they were fulfilling their destinies to hit, mutilate and maim humanity. As we ran toward them, these guys would start screaming and laughing, and then they unloaded on us with the impact of a car crash. That drill turned into a virtual slaughterhouse. Never had I been beaten up so thoroughly in such a short period of time. My nose, which was slightly accessible through the cage, was gushing blood; my lower lip was nearly ripped in two; and there wasn't a portion of my body that wasn't bruised and aching by the end of the drill. Saban had proven his point at the cost of a couple of receivers, but the guys left definitely had a different perspective on blocking.

I phoned my wife that evening, exhausted and beat up, and told her I didn't know how much longer I could take these physically exhausting workouts. Maybe Saban was running us too hard. My anguish didn't come from the bodily pain. It came from the fear and anticipation of the next day's practice, not knowing if I could push myself to the physical limit that was being demanded of us during this trial period.

Since this was the most strenuous training camp that any of the Buffalo Bills could remember, we all began to develop more respect and compassion for each other. I guess you could call it a military boot camp mentality that toughens up all the recruits and soldiers into a machine that wants to win. The players who were spilling their blood and giving their all on the practice field were bonding together into a mutual-admiration society. Friendships off the field were springing up between men who, while not necessarily the best players, were the ones who just wouldn't quit or back down when things got tough. The difference between this year and last was incredible, as I recalled how everyone then was ready to quit by the second or third quarter. Because we were losing, we'd just run out of steam because nobody gave a damn. Being a winner is not something that just comes naturally; it's taught and nurtured. It comes from a respect that one develops for oneself. With the attitude that Saban was instilling in all of us at training camp, I imagined that, win or lose, this team and its players would be coming at you for sixty minutes. If they didn't, they wouldn't be around on Monday to talk about it.

Saban's realism was encouraging. He had no illusions about performing a miracle to turn the team around in one season. His three-step plan was to make the Bills a credible team this season, a competitive team the next season, and hopefully win our division that third season. First, he started cleaning house on what had been the Buffalo Bills for the past three to five years. When a coach comes in to rebuild, the hatchet falls hard and frequently. Saban not only had to change players, he had to change the personality of the team. After a team has lost continually for several years, even the good players forget how to win.

It was scary but, at the same time, exhilarating. I was running myself to exhaustion and getting knocked around like a bumper car, but I kept coming back because I wanted very much to be a part of this new feeling. By the end of that season, Saban had turned over about 30 percent of our team. But the guys who remained were filled with the most incredible esprit de corps and were ready to show the NFL that the Buffalo Bills were no longer a laughing matter.

The season started uneventfully. We lost a couple of games, but we weren't shut out as in years past. The exciting part was that our offense started scoring some points, and it was at this time that O. J. Simpson began to come into his own.

Saban was still an enigma to me. At times, he could be the sweetest and gentlest man in football, but then turn into the meanest bastard imaginable. On Monday morning—if we weren't playing a Monday game—he would usually run game films from the day before. If it was a particularly bad game, Saban would stand before running the projector, and very slowly he would fill with anger as he spoke to us. I always sat in front because his idiosyncrasies fascinated me. He would clench and unclench his fists as he sank lower and lower into almost a lineman's hitting stance. Maybe it was my imagination, but his tinted glasses seemed to get darker as he became more angry and his face grew redder. He would finally erupt like a geyser and scare all of us out of our minds. While he was spewing forth on what was wrong with us, he'd yank the reel of film out of the projector and throw it against the wall. The reel would break apart and the loops of celluloid would unwind and fall all over the place. Coach Saban had proved his point: we didn't need to go over the mistakes we made in that game. We all felt so intimidated that we mentally vowed to ourselves that we weren't going to allow Saban to get this worked up again; therefore, we'd work even harder not to screw up the next time. Saban's psychology worked. He had found the right combination of compassion, fear, anger and honesty that endeared his players to him and his style of football. The last thing we wanted to do was let him down.

This season marked the last time that we played at War Memorial Stadium. We no longer practiced at the Amherst Recreation Center because Saban felt we could live happily ever after without stumbling on concrete dividers. Instead, we practiced in a cow pasture behind a motel about twenty miles south of Buffalo. I moved into a place nearby called the Buffalo South Exit 56 Motel, which was a truck stop across the thruway. Even though I was a second-year player, I still had no fantasies about my station in life. Huge semis would pull up and rumble outside my door throughout the night, and the neon signs would blink in my window. The motel had a little restaurant called Grandma's where I would eat most of my meals amidst the truckers.

Even though I was close to many of my teammates, I still hadn't formed any tight friendships. I suppose I was still smarting from the anger I felt when my best friend from my rookie year, Busty Underwood, was cut from the team early in the season. To show you how your mind can distort situations, I actually thought that Busty wouldn't get cut because Saban liked me so much that he wouldn't want to hurt my feelings. I, therefore, felt that the coach would bend over backward before getting rid of Busty—if only as a gesture to show his appreciation of me. That may sound like wacky logic now, but at the time, it made perfect sense to me. The team destroyed a relationship without consulting me, and it just didn't seem fair. So, on the day that Busty got cut, I went around acting very angry and sullen, hoping that the staff would put it together that I was pissed off about losing my best friend. Needless to say, neither Saban nor any member of his staff caught my drift, as they say. For all they noticed, I might have been walking around all day with a bad case of heartburn. Hurt feelings were not a concern in professional football.

At season's end, I was again grateful that I hadn't suffered any serious injury, especially since I was now blocking those not-so-puny safeties and linebackers. Lou Saban had given me my first taste of what professional football was really like, and I couldn't wait for next season.

When I returned to California before Christmas, Marilyn and I decided to buy a house which she had found in my hometown of Whittier. I was feeling so excited about surviving a second season intact that I welcomed a thirty-year mortgage, as I figured I'd be playing for many more years. Symbolically, the house was also important to us as a married couple. Since our life together lasted only half the year, we needed some roots to give our marriage a sense of permanence.

After moving in, I decided to spend part of my off-season painting the house all by myself. Having never done this before, I felt pressured to do a good job, especially since my father, who was an expert painter himself, was casually overseeing my work. I even learned how to hang wallpaper. Somehow or other, it took me the whole damn off-season to finish the house, and it wasn't a terribly large house at that. I had become so used to living a physical existence that the painting seemed like a natural extension of it. My manual-work output seemed to fill the time, and I didn't realize that it was almost a year since I had properly utilized that organ between my ears.

Marilyn and I began to feel strains in our relationship. I guess it was the usual period of adjustment for most newlyweds, but ours was unique in that we had lived apart for half a year. Busily getting her teaching credentials, Marilyn had organized a certain rhythm to her life, and she was beginning to resent having a husband around the house all the time, whether he was painting or loafing. I was pissed off at her resentment, yet by early July, I knew in the deepest recess of my mind that I had chosen to totally waste the past six months of my life. I was determined never to let that happen again, and by the time I flew east to training camp in mid-July, Marilyn and I had mended our differences, and we were truly sorry about leaving each other once again.

The weeks at training camp went smoothly, and I'm not sure whether it was Coach Saban's influence or the fact that we would baptize our new stadium that season, but something made me feel that the Buffalo Bills were at last falling into place. I actually felt good enough about myself that I no longer wanted to live masochistically in the Buffalo South Exit 56 Motel. For me, it was a milestone to move into an apartment with a newly acquired friend and teammate, Leo Hart. To make sure that I didn't get homesick for my former residence, we managed to find a place adjacent to the tollbooths of the New York Thruway.

It just happened to be the best of all times to be living in Buffalo. The city was undergoing a renaissance of civic pride primarily because of the new stadium, which was considered one of the country's best. The owner of a local dairy paid a reported million dollars to have the 80,000-seat facility named after him, and poetically enough, his name was Mr. Rich. Ironically, you could barely see the tiny letters that spelled out "Rich" on the building's exterior, and it seemed like all of the local media referred to it as "Buffalo Bills' Stadium." Considering upstate New York's ridiculously bad winters, I was always surprised that for some political or economical reason they didn't put a dome on it. But that was the only criticism I had for the place. The locker rooms were luxurious, and we could've spent hours in the shower before running out of hot water. There was a TV lounge where we'd sit around before practice and watch reruns of *Gunsmoke* and *The Rifleman*. Besides having the luxury of a sauna, we also had an indoor basketball court and even two racquetball courts. I would loosen up every day playing racquetball, and when it was particularly cold, and we couldn't do much throwing, Joe Ferguson, our new quarterback, and I would go down on the court after practice and throw for about half an hour. For those of us who'd never played for any other team, we began to feel like we were playing for the first time in the pros.

As if to show the city that we were worthy of such luxurious surroundings, we took off at a gallop, although we sputtered a bit on the opening kickoff. Picture this: 80,000 screaming halfdrunk fans, proud of their new stadium and hungry for a win, were on their feet for the kickoff in this premiere game against the Washington Redskins. John Leypoldt kicked it deep, and Washington ran it back 97 yards for a touchdown. While we were shocked, the fans were stunned. This upbeat moment had instantly become that sinking, "Oh no, not again!" But we regrouped and were rapidly becoming a team to be reckoned with that year.

Being almost prescient before our first game, Saban changed the team's symbol from a stationary buffalo to one that was charging and looked like it could easily pick up a third and one! We also had tremendous help from a great draft. Players such as Joe DeLamielleure, Reggie McKenzie, and Paul Seymore—all of whom were offensive linemen brought in to clear the way for O.J. to gain 2,003 yards that year! J. D. Hill and I were the two starting receivers, and I must confess that I became a fan favorite, partly for my playing on the field and partly because I was white. The sports fans in Buffalo were predominantly white, blue-collar workers in 1973, and it was much easier for them to identify with me than, say, a superstar like Simpson. The Juice made Buffalo something very special, but no matter how hard he tried to be one of them, the truth was, the city was just borrowing O.J. for a while.

Buffalo was truly beginning to grow on me, and I realized that much of that was due to my becoming well known in the city. We were starting to do something that the people never expected: win games! Leo Hart and I would go out on the town every night to eat in restaurants and drop in some bars for a few beers. Unlike years past when some of the fans wanted to lynch us on sight, the people of Buffalo now welcomed us with open arms. Since I had never before been treated to the adulation accorded someone like Simpson, I began to relish my own notoriety and quietly enjoyed being recognized and signing autographs. It only took two and a half years and a lot of aches and pain for me to recapture that "big-man-on-campus" feeling I had had at USC.

Speaking of pain, it was something I was becoming accustomed to. I was developing a chronic low-back pain, and my knees began to ache from the constant high-speed torquing that was required of them.

The season's third game, which we played in San Diego, was my first chance to show off in front of my friends and family, who had driven down from Los Angeles. In the third quarter, I ran a slant pattern. That's a quick hitting route where you try to make a catch between the corner and the safety before one or the other takes your head off. The ball was thrown high, actually too high to ever catch, but being young and fearless, I went up for it. The strong safety hit me low, and I did a full flip. When I completed my circle, my leg hit first and hyperextended. When I got up, I knew something was wrong, but I wasn't about to let it stop me just when things were getting good.

After about a half hour of commiserating with my wife and folks after the game, I flew with the team back to Buffalo, where I was scheduled to have an arthrogram the following morning.

The machine used for doing arthrograms looks somewhat like a medieval torture device. After receiving a local anesthetic, a four-inch needle is inserted into the kneecap which sends a dye into all the cavities of the entire knee joint. Then, a battery of x-rays is taken, while the knee is stressed by the doctor, and finally the same needle is used to drain out the dye and any other fluid that has accumulated in the swollen knee. This diagnostic procedure is even more painful than the actual injury.

I was learning how incredibly complex and finely tuned our bodies are. When anything goes wrong in the knee, nature solidifies the joint with fluid to keep it from as much movement as possible. This is part of the healing process unless you happen to be playing in the NFL, in which case the fluid is drained off the knee with little regard for mother nature.

I made up my mind that I wasn't going to quit playing that season just because of a swollen knee. I couldn't! It happened to be the first time that I was leading my team in receiving. No longer worried about being cut, I was becoming an integral part of this winning machine. I felt I was as good as anyone in the league, and for the very first time, I had a coach who had now become a friend of mine. Lou Saban would actually call on me at meetings, asking my opinion of various patterns and finding out what I could and couldn't do. While being concerned as hell about my bum knee, Saban also knew me well enough to know that I was going to keep playing and finish the season.

But the pain in my knee was becoming incredible. At that time, pain-killing drugs weren't common—particularly under the aegis of Dr. Godfrey, our team physician, who was an excellent doctor and as conservative as they come. He would give me aspirin for the pain during the week, and just before the game and during half time, he would dispense one Empirin with codeine. Meanwhile, I caught a total of thirty-three passes that season, and after undergoing three separate arthrograms, nobody still knew what exactly was happening with my knee.

One of the reasons I kept a sense of humor that season during the ordeal of my knee was because of a teammate named Dave

Costa. A veteran for years, Costa became the team's resident court jester. This guy had long hair, a full beard, and so much hair on his body that he looked like a grizzly bear in the locker room. At the team's Halloween party, Costa arrived with a little towel wrapped around his middle. He had shaved exactly one half of his body, from his half-bald scalp to his half beard, to his clean-shaven arm, chest and leg. When he stood sideways, he looked like either a bald, hairless eunuch or the wolfman. This guy did these crazy things all season long, and he was always screaming and laughing. There were no restrictions on having beards at that time, and Saban let any guy do what he wanted. Some of my teammates thought Costa was certifiable, while in reality he was just an overgrown kid who had a great time by disregarding his inhibitions. He would come to an interview wearing those giant dime-store sunglasses with the price tag hanging out in front and he would be dead serious. He put on everybody, from the team's owner to reporters to Saban himself. While watching Costa perform some of his crazy stunts, I would become envious, wishing that I wasn't so laid-back and predictable.

Dr. Godfrey wanted me to have exploratory knee surgery in Buffalo as soon as we played our last game. I told him that I wanted to have the surgery in Los Angeles so I could be home with my wife. Since this was my first knee surgery, I had to psych myself up for it. On too many occasions, I'd heard or read about one knee surgery ending a man's playing career. And it's not so much the injury itself that is so debilitating; rather, it's the effort to overcome the mental anguish that always accompanies knee operations. It's the fear that you may not be able to perform as you used to, or worse still, the anxiety about hurting that knee again. My own style of running patterns was based on my ability to make radical cuts and twists that really take a toll on your knees, and since I never had that gift of great speed that some receivers have, this was an essential part of my game.

Before having surgery, I had decided that I would find a law school that would accommodate my kind of part-time program and get started. This decision was partly due, I'm sure, to my doubts about being able to play well again and also because I had vowed by then to make my off-seasons as demanding mentally for me as my football seasons had become for me physically. A small, relatively unknown law school, Western State, accepted me and worked out a special program where I would attend only during the spring semesters. With that professional insurance under my belt, I wanted to get that knee operation over with as quickly as possible, and get on the road to recovery.

Deep down in her heart, I'm sure Marilyn was hoping I'd come through the surgery successfully and, then, quit while I was still in one piece and become an attorney. That definitely wasn't my plan of action. I convinced myself that I would come through the operation with flying colors because, at that time, I had blind faith in the medical profession and in my body as well. When you're young and strong, you feel indestructible. Your thoughts are, if something does happen to break, don't worry, because it'll heal. The fallacy is you can only put your body and mind through this mental exercise so many times.

As I began to fall asleep under the anesthetic, I was wondering why my wife wasn't as optimistic as I was that everything was going to be all right forever after.

5

Buffalo's Electric Company Lights the Way—The Golden Years

It comes in funny shapes resembling a
sphere,
As it whistles toward you humming
a quaint little song of fear.
It begins its travel, suspended
like bait,
With little regard for its eventual
fate.
Its independent nature renders an
erratic path,
Which sends would-be trappers
to an early bath.
This odd-shaped little pigskin is
often caught,
But don't get brash, because then again,
it's often not!

—BOB CHANDLER
1975—Essex Hotel
New York, New York
The night before the game.

Awakening in the hospital room with a cast nudging into my groin, I saw Marilyn smiling at me from across the room. She said, "The good news is that you still have a leg!" The bad news turned out to be that they had to remove the medial meniscus, which is the cartilage on the outside of the knee, while cutting out the anterior cruciate ligament, which was snapped in two and rolled up like a window shade. So I had had the "Joe Namath" operation, I mused, wondering if I'd ever play well enough again for the surgery to be renamed in my honor. Although the doctors told me that the healing would be fast, we all feared that my knee would never regain its total strength. Would it ever be able to take the punishment I'd been giving it every Sunday?

I didn't get out of the hospital for about a week, and in the meantime, Marilyn bought my law books and went to the introductory class for me. For the next few weeks, she would drop me off at school because the cast was so big that I couldn't possibly get behind the driver's seat.

And that was how I started my career at law school—the fallen warrior. Nobody recognized my name that semester, and no one pressed me beyond the explanation of knee surgery. I kind of enjoyed my anonymity because I wasn't too sure if I was going to do well. I had been concentrating on X's and O's for so long that it took me a few days just to get used to the written word.

After six weeks, the cast was removed, and I mounted a campaign to rehabilitate my knee as soon as possible. Now being able to drive, I would go over to a gym in Anaheim every day after classes and would go through the slow, laborious process of strengthening the knee with incremental weights. Every once in a while the knee would swell up, but my doctors told me that this was normal, so I would just let the joint rest for a few days while my body absorbed the fluid. I went into a panic after every episode of swelling because it always happened unexpectedly and came upon me with no warning. I had this fantasy that in the middle of a game next season, the TV announcer would exclaim, "As Bob Chandler jumped to catch the pass, his knee popped out like a hot-air balloon, and it's carrying him higher and higher until, we regret to say, he's no longer within the range of our cameras."

Compensating for my unpredictable knee was the fact that I

did fairly well on my exams at the end of May. Marilyn was positively ecstatic over the results, especially since she had suspicions that my mind had gotten scrambled inside my helmet. This was the very first time in my life that I had concentrated on my studies, and it was an entirely new experience for me. But most amazing of all, I felt as much satisfaction walking out of my law school finals as I did after having a great game.

When I got back to the training camp outside of Buffalo, I learned that the Bills had traded Dennis Shaw to St. Louis for Ahmad Rashad. Formerly known as Bobby Moore, from the University of Oregon, Rashad was a superb wide receiver who was erroneously thought to be a malcontent in St. Louis. Now, the team had me, J. D. Hill and Rashad—probably three of the better receivers in the league—but they only had two spots to play. While I thought the team was justified in picking up Rashad, considering my knee surgery, I verged on paranoia, hoping that my quirky knee wouldn't make me the odd man out.

In that particular year, fate had a way of intervening and postponing my plight. Before any of us had a chance to start training camp, the NFL went on strike. It was the fall of 1974, when the players' war cry was, "No freedom, no football!" What it really boiled down to was that when a player played out his contract, he wanted to be a free agent to have other teams bid for his services and go to whichever team he chose. At the time, it seemed like we were galley slaves chained to our oars on some Roman warship.

All the NFL players were organized in some loose kind of union called the Players Association, which was recognized by the AFL-CIO; but the lines of communication between players and teams broke down, forcing us to find out what was happening by reading the newspapers. Ed Garvey, who was head of the Players Association at the time, convinced almost everyone to boycott training camp. The guys who didn't were mainly the rookies and first-year players who were scared shitless of losing out on what slim chance they had.

By this time, all of the veterans had grown to hate training camp, which was probably a big motivation behind the strike. We figured, what the hell, why not take off for a few weeks and let this thing just blow over. To keep from turning into mush, we would work out daily at a local community college where lots of people would come to watch. These workouts turned out to be completely half-assed, where we all seemed to be marching to a different drummer.

Meanwhile, the players in training camp were starting exhibition games with makeshift rosters. As for me, I had been getting a little tired of just goofing off. While I was still nervous about my knee acting up, I wanted a chance to play on it and put it to the test.

That test came earlier than expected. One afternoon at Erie Community College, I was running a route, and suddenly I felt a stabbing pain on both the outside and the inside of my knee. Within hours, my knee swelled up like a grapefruit, and I could just barely move it. "Way to go, jerk," I cursed to myself, wondering what the hell I had done. The paranoia that I had shut out earlier now came pouring down on me in torrents. I kept thinking that one damn knee surgery was all it took to retire one Robert Chandler at the peak of his career. As I was feeling sorry for myself, I thought about the injustice of it all; there I was limping around with a cane while Rashad and Hill were running and jumping like gazelles on the field.

My nightly phone calls to Marilyn became succeedingly more morose. It was bad enough that I wasn't getting paid because of the strike, but the bad knee on top of it all was more than I could handle. I was beginning to lose sleep at night worrying about whether I'd be playing my swan song this year.

Using a very clever tactic, management helped to break the strike. They would call a player's home during the day, and when the wife answered, they would say something to the effect of, "Jeez, if your husband doesn't come in, it doesn't look good. Guess we'll have to make plans with some other players." That's all the guy needed. Presumably, the player had moved to Buffalo with wife and kids, and now their collective future in the city was uncertain. The wife would then keep bugging the player until he agreed to cross the picket line.

O. J. Simpson was another story altogether. Despite his negative feelings about the union leadership, because he felt that they had misled him in a promotional deal a few years earlier, he still supported the strike and his fellow players, and held out until nearly every other team member had capitulated.

The entire strike turned out to be an exercise in futility, since we began playing without a contract, only an agreement in principle, and it would take about three more years before the union eventually signed the contract. In effect, we sold ourselves down the river regarding our "freedom." Any team that took a free-agent player would be forced to compensate the new team according to a schedule relating to the player's salary. Therefore, typical compensation for a good player might be something like a first- and second-round draft choice, which no team was likely to give up. In fact, it became obvious that collusion among the owners rendered 99 percent of the free agents without a bid from any team in the NFL.

Lou Saban was none too happy about most of the team starting so late. His three-year game plan never considered the possibility of a strike. Consequently, he worked us harder than ever before to get into shape quickly.

My knee was a mess. Every time I would run hard on it during practice, it would balloon up and hurt like hell. Dr. Godfrey examined it thoroughly and decided I had what was known in the medical trade as a Baker's cyst. (No one ever told me what the poor bastard named Baker did to deserve this immortality.) The irritation of the knee joint from the surgery caused this cyst to grow inside. The cyst was the culprit that caused the knee to swell so badly, and after more evaluation, Godfrey told me that the only way to mitigate the problem was having another operation to remove it.

Mentally, I just couldn't face more surgery at that time. I was anxious to play some football no matter what kind of shape my knee was in. The season started, and because of the injury,

Rashad had taken my spot on the roster. Had he not been there, I suppose Saban would grudgingly have let me play on Sundays and simply rest me during the week. Now, I would go in to hold the ball for field goals and extra points; and whenever they needed a third wide receiver, which was infrequently, I was sent in. I was the "spare tire" that Saban had on hand in case anything happened to Hill or Rashad.

Looking back, I believe that here was my first big mistake. I began abusing my knee, which would later prove to be very costly. I should have had the surgery immediately and spent the balance of the season rehabilitating. Had I done this, my knee would have suffered far less trauma. Instead, I decided to "tough it out" and be ready to take over when needed. As it turned out I actually gave up the year anyway and still managed to inflame my knee every day during practice. Boy, was I stupid! But what was really killing me was the thought that all of Buffalo believed I had gotten beat out by better players, rather than by an injury.

It was all part of my screwed-up pattern of always having to prove myself. I knew damn well that Saban knew my talent and had appreciated my performance during the past two seasons. But somehow in my unconscious mind I felt I was letting him down by going on sick leave. In every restaurant or bar that I went to, I found myself trying to convince the fans that I was hurt and didn't get beat out of my starting job. Making matters worse for me was the fact that Saban's plan was working. The Bills were winning games, and what was later to be called "The Electric Company" (our offensive linemen sparked by O. J. Simpson) was ranked as the number-one offense in the National Football League.

Things were even rotten on a personal level. Leo Hart and I had planned to get another apartment together this season. While we were looking for a place to live in the early part of the season, we would also go out every night and have a few beers. I wasn't playing because of my knee, and Leo wasn't playing either, since he was the backup quarterback. We finally found a terrific apartment in town, and just as we were about to sublet it,

Leo was cut from the team. My luck was so bad that I even lost my best friend on the team. I was so devastated that I lost my incentive to take the apartment myself, and before long I was back at the Buffalo South Exit 56 Motel, where the truckers welcomed me back with open arms. That place's depressing atmosphere suited my mood perfectly.

Talk about ambivalence! On the one hand, I was genuinely delighted that the Buffalo Bills had reached the playoffs at season's end. Conversely, I couldn't stand the fact that I wasn't a big part of the team's success. In our first playoff game, we lost to Pittsburgh, which ended our season.

All the rest of our players took off after the game, and I spent the evening having dinner with Gerry Mullins, a guard for the Steelers, who had been one of my roommates back at USC. After I told Gerry that I was staying in Buffalo for a week longer in order to have Dr. Godfrey operate on my knee, he took pity on me and convinced me to at least spend Christmas with him in Pittsburgh.

What an unforgettable Christmas that was! Besides being forced to socialize with some of the Steelers, who were jubilant over beating the Bills, I was terribly lonesome for Marilyn, my folks, and a southern California Christmas. After a day, I just couldn't stand being in Pittsburgh any longer, so I borrowed Gerry's car and decided to drive to New York City. I suppose I felt I would mesh more easily in the anonymity of the Big Apple, where I knew absolutely no one. It was snowing like hell as I maneuvered the Pennsylvania Turnpike, and it took me twice as long to reach Manhattan. After checking into the Americana Hotel, I felt miserable and figured out about two hours later that I had come down with the flu. That night was Christmas Eve, and there I was alone in my hotel room feeling too lousy to even have room service bring me dinner. I phoned Marilyn and spent a long time commiserating over the fact that we were both alone and three thousand miles apart on that December 24 evening. The next day, I stayed in my room drinking juices to kick the flu, and even though I still felt very weak, I decided to drive back to

Pittsburgh to return Gerry's car and get back to Buffalo to get this operation over with. On this trip, it was snowing so hard that I was forced to pull over a couple of times and wait for the snowplows.

When I arrived in Pittsburgh, Gerry informed me that the airport had closed down. As a last recourse, I took an overnight Greyhound bus, which got me to Buffalo the following morning. Going straight to the hospital, I was told that I couldn't have the surgery until my fever went down. And so I checked into my home away from home, the Buffalo South Exit 56 Motel, and spent three more days trying to drown my fever with liquids.

Finally, back in the hospital I was operated on by Dr. Godfrey, who removed the Baker's cyst and sewed up a hole in my knee capsule that had been overlooked during the first surgery. After spending New Year's Eve in the hospital and twelve subsequent days in bed, I struggled to get on board an American Airlines flight, where they allowed me to place my cast-encased leg on a crate.

Nothing could have cheered me more than seeing Marilyn waiting for me at the LA airport. My experience of that Christmas really set my priorities straight, and we made a pact to try and spend the holidays together the rest of our lives (unless, of course, we ever got into the playoffs again).

Once again, Marilyn became my driver as I hustled over to the law school to catch up with the two weeks I'd missed when the semester began. I thought maybe the teachers and students were getting a little tired of seeing me arrive late and in plaster up to my ass. I took a heavier load that term and again did relatively well. And this time, I very slowly worked on the knee after the cast was removed. I swore I'd take no more chances until it felt right.

The afternoon workouts increased as the months went by and the knee never swelled. Not even once. In fact, the knee felt as strong as ever. You would've thought that I died and went to heaven from the way I kept smiling all the time. I had actually gotten a reprieve, and if my luck held out, I might even have a few more seasons in me.

Because I was feeling so good about myself, I decided I needed a reward. So I went out and did something I had never done before—purchased a magnificent, new Porsche 911S. Putting such a large amount of money into that automobile was completely off the wall for me. Having overcome the ridiculous adversity of the previous year, I guess I felt like a winner at last, and therefore was going to look like one, no matter what the cost.

As soon as school was over, Marilyn and I drove across country in our new buggy. We had nearly a month to meander, and it turned out to be one of our best times together. I'll admit I was damned difficult to live with when I first got back in January. I was grouchy as hell, and it was all part of my feeling sorry for myself. Marilyn is not the most sympathetic person in the world, but somehow her ambivalence forced me not to feel sorry for myself and to get well. We spent some extra time in North Carolina where Marilyn could visit her grandmother, and where we later had a great reunion with Leo Hart and his wife. After Marilyn flew back to California, I drove up to New York City alone.

Remembering those grim days and nights spent at the Americana last Christmas, I shuddered as I drove through the city. But I was a new person now and wanted everyone to know it. Impulsively, I stopped at a fancy hair salon and got a permanent. Even though I knew I'd be taking an awful ribbing when my teammates saw my new curly locks, it was time for a new image. (The curls became so popular that I was later asked to pose for a local salon's ad to convince prospective male customers that getting a permanent wave was a manly thing to do.)

Looking like Apollo in his chariot, I drove to training camp while feeling on top of the world. Saban was delighted about my recovery, and I silently prayed that I would stay healthy and not disappoint him this season.

Training camp is a drudgery no matter what team you're playing for. Some teams make it much more enjoyable, but it's still a lot of hard work. A typical day begins at 7:00 A.M. with a crashing bang on the door by one of the ball boys. After a mandatory breakfast, you're on the field at 9:00 A.M. in full gear. (This is just about the time that all your joints are beginning to semi-function.) The two-hour practice is followed by weightlifting, then a shower, which is followed by treatment for aches and pains. Following a noon lunch, we'd spend an hour sleeping or watching soap operas. (Incidentally, most NFL players can tell you everything you'd want to know about *All My Children*.) After loosening up and getting taped in the training room, we'd be out on the field in full gear again by 3:00 P.M. Two and a half hours and about ten miles of running later, you drag yourself into the training room for more treatment and a shower before a 6:00 dinner. If you eat very fast, you might even catch a quick beer between dinner and the 7:00 P.M. meeting that would last about two hours. Between 9:00 and 9:30 P.M., you're free to do anything you want until 11:00 P.M., which is curfew.

Training camp is definitely the dress rehearsal for the regular season. Gradually, the workload is cut down considerably by September. You're still expected to maintain your conditioning and remain mentally alert, but you must now police yourself when it comes to hours and night life.

It was such a pleasure to work out and practice with J. D. Hill and Rashad—and to consider myself their equal during those early weeks. Because of last season, I was down to number three on the list of receivers, but I knew that a healthy Bob Chandler could not be kept out of the starting lineup.

Marilyn flew into Buffalo to spend a week with me just prior to our first exhibition game. On the night before the game, Rashad and his wife, Tillie, joined us for dessert at the Friendly Ice Cream Shop. Ahmad was in rare form that night, keeping all of us at the table laughing continuously. He was describing his philosophy of always playing football injury-free. It was so comical to hear this guy, who had so much talent, talk about not going over the middle or extending himself too far for a pass. I mean, Rashad was so big and fast that he could literally be playing at 80 percent of capacity and still be sensational. In comparison, my wide-receiving style, which focused on an almost acrobatic "sacrificing-my-body" type of play, was done because I wasn't physically as gifted.

Ironically, Rashad and I both started next night's exhibition game, but our potent combo was short-lived. Rashad tore his knee to shreds, which put him out for the whole season. I remember going to the hospital to visit him a few days after his surgery, and the poor guy seemed to be shellshocked. With all of his talent, he had been blessed with never having anything serious happen to him on the field, and he was finding it very difficult to deal with.

Having two combat medals from my own bouts with it, I was something of an authority on knee surgery. Initially the pain is so excruciating that you almost wish your leg would fall off. Then, it gets worse when the knee starts swelling inside the cast. On top of all that, Ahmad had developed an infection and was running a fever. With sweat pouring off his face, he looked at me and said, "I'll never play this game again!" He was suffering from the reality syndrome that accompanies every serious injury. With a guy like me, it would last a couple weeks—for Rashad, it lasted for four months. I tried to goad him into retracting what he was saying. He smiled through his pain and said, "Bullshit! I'm never stepping back on that field again, because I will never go through this again."

After Rashad's untimely injury, Hill and I started for the Bills that year. What a year it was for me! Second in the league in receiving, I caught fifty-five passes. But there was still a price to pay. By midseason, my chin required six stitches after it had been torn open, one of my front teeth had been knocked out, both elbows had become so bruised that they swelled up and had to be drained weekly, and, last but not least, my lung had burst after being hit in the back with a helmet while reaching for a high pass. It was in the third quarter against Denver on an unseasonably warm Sunday afternoon in October at Rich Stadium. I ran an out pattern; the ball was thrown high and a little bit behind me. As I stretched to catch the ball, Ken Reaves, Denver's corner, hit me with his helmet square in the back. Having the wind knocked out of me was nothing unusual, so I didn't pay any attention to it. I jogged off the field and sat down as the punting team came in on fourth down.

When I got up to go back on the field a few minutes later, I felt something moving up and down inside my chest. Good God, I thought the impact had knocked my heart loose. Dr. Godfrey took my pulse, which was racing at about 180 beats per minute. Taking me immediately inside and laying me down on a table, he was able to make my heart rate slow down. I was then taken to the hospital where x-rays showed that no ribs were cracked or fractured. I was released, and although still in a good deal of pain, I managed to go out and celebrate our win until 4:00 A.M. One of my good friends from college, Rich Whitman, had flown in for the weekend and I didn't want to sissy out and go home to bed. As it turned out, Rich had a helluva time spending the wee hours with a young lady who had just left a convent.

Rich had to catch an early flight back to LA the next morning. When he came to wake me up for a ride, I told him I couldn't get out of bed because I felt so lousy. I asked Rich if he would mind taking a cab, which he didn't, and I crawled out of bed about six hours later.

Returning to the stadium that afternoon, I tried running again, and whatever had been knocked loose was still moving around in my chest. Insisting that they send me to a heart specialist, I wound up being examined by one of Buffalo's best, who took yet another battery of x-rays.

His diagnosis was that my left lung had collapsed. I was taken to the hospital's emergency room where a chest specialist placed an oversized needle in my chest to free the trapped air and permit my lung to reinflate to its normal position.

As it turned out, the heart specialist wasn't a season-ticket holder, and therefore he warned me to wait at least four weeks before starting to play. The thoracic surgeon, however, was a diehard Bills fan, and he said that I would be ready to play in five days! It goes without saying that I took the advice of the chest man, and I was playing the following Sunday.

I had another reason to get well fast because that night was our annual rookie party. The rookie party is usually held after training camp, but we were making so many player changes at that time that we decided to hold off until we knew who was going to be around for possibly the rest of the season.

The party was held in a private banquet room at one of the hotels in the Buffalo area. The half dozen or so rookies we had that season had worked out an agenda and procured the talent for the evening. It goes without saying that wives and girlfriends were forbidden to attend.

First on the menu was a fancy dinner washed down with much wine and beer. After a few hours, everyone was very loose and looking forward to what the evening held in store. Little did we know that the waitresses were indeed working girls—but they weren't accustomed to waiting on tables or working standing up. No one really caught on to the real identity of these ladies until one of them was served up for dessert. (After a few bottles of wine, it's amazing how fast some guys will lose their inhibitions. Incredibly, nine times out of ten, it's the guy you'd never expect who ends up being the wildest.)

After the ice was broken, or should I say, the dessert was eaten, all hell broke loose. Now, mind you, in my sensitive condition, I was under doctor's orders to stay relaxed and refrain from any activity that would raise my blood pressure. So, I was relegated to the role of spectator which was, no doubt, the safest position.

Initially, most of the guys were engrossed watching two girls getting to know each other intimately while yelling that they could do it better. As the natives got more restless, they started ushering young ladies from the bar downstairs into our little private party. They came as willing victims; after all, doesn't every girl want to attend at least one NFL party in her life?

One of the veteran players on our team was famous for the measure of his manhood. Let's put it this way: It was so long in its limp state that he could tie it in a knot. Anyway, we noticed this wily veteran snuggling up to a somewhat unsuspecting groupie. I say unsuspecting because although they both had the same thing in mind, she had *no* idea what kind of anatomical delight the evening held in store.

There were certain rooms that were made available to us, and naturally on a seniority basis. My roommate told this player that some of his buddies had bets on whether the girl would have room to accommodate his pet monster without getting killed in the process. In order to protect our bets, we naturally had to watch the action. Knowing that the girl would never agree to an audience, we told him to give us a few minutes, and we'd position ourselves in the closet. Now, imagine four horny, drunken football players crammed into a hotel closet like high school kids getting their first look at sex.

The only thing we heard out of the poor girl was, "Oh my God," and then one of the guys fell through the closet door right into the bedroom. The young lady grabbed her clothes, left her shoes, and ran down the hall screaming her lungs out. To this day, we never knew if she was running from us or from his secret weapon!

There were a lot of bloodshot eyes at practice the next morning, but also quite a few wry smiles and a library of stories to be told for years to come.

Although still living at the Exit 56 Motel, I had become very close to Tony Greene, an All-Pro free safety, who had an apartment in town. Every night, I would drive my Porsche to Tony's and then we'd go out and really live it up in Buffalo. We got to know a lot of the people in town, and we built up a tremendous camaraderie with most of them.

Every now and then, we'd meet some belligerent bozo who wanted to put us down. I remember one snowy night in November when Tony and I were in this bar called Schoney's, and the guy sitting next to me was getting drunker and more belligerent by the minute. He started bugging me by comparing himself to me and saying that he should be earning what I was paid. After eight beers, I put a fifty-dollar bill down on the bar and told this guy to put his money where his mouth was. He'd been bragging that he was faster than me, so I told him that we should race out in the parking lot for the fifty bucks. I was actually joking, but he jumped at the chance. Tony told me what a stupid son of a bitch I was as we all assembled in the icy parking lot. We raced about sixty yards, and I left this guy at the starting gate where he slipped on the ice about five yards out. I took his fifty dollars and bought everyone in the house a beer.

I got to enjoy the regime of playing hard during the day and going out to raise hell every night. We particularly liked Mulligan's Cafe, a new club that had opened that year and was packed every night. It was really life in the fast lane—as fast as it can be in Buffalo. Tony and I were always recognized wherever we went, which gave me a real sense of self-satisfaction. Women all seemed to be fascinated by football players, and most knew or suspected that I was married, but that didn't seem to concern them very much. Although attractive women were readily available, the chase was much more exciting than the catch.

As the season wound down, it was apparent that the Bills wouldn't get to the playoffs that year. I felt bad for the team, but simultaneously I felt good about my performance that season. In addition, I figured that I had a chance to be selected for the Pro Bowl. All the players and coaches in the NFL vote for the Pro Bowl, with the only stipulation being that you can't vote for any player on your own team. Four wide receivers were to be chosen, and I was sure that I'd make it, since I was second in the AFC in receptions. Unfortunately, not enough players felt as I did, and I was fifth in the voting. I was able to console myself by knowing that my own teammates felt I had deserved it and, most importantly, respected my talents as a player. If they thought I was the best, then it really didn't matter if I received any other honors elsewhere—I guess.

Driving my Porsche back to California, I amazed myself by how excited I was to be getting back to law school. Even though I had a fine season, I was now looking forward to a strictly mental existence. I thought about many things during that long drive across the country, particularly about Marilyn and me. Despite the economic riskiness of playing pro ball, I wanted to improve the quality of life for us. It was then that I decided that we should get a larger home.

Right off the bat, we sold our $35,000 house for $70,000.

Using our small windfall as a down payment, we were able to buy a home in the best part of Whittier for $95,000. The first two nights after the closing, Marilyn and I couldn't sleep, thinking that we'd gone crazy and were in way over our heads. The new house was twice the size of our old one, and no sooner did we move in than we financed building a pool and a Jacuzzi. I think unconsciously I wanted a nicer house to give Marilyn something to look forward to as I took off for another season. With so much house, our respective parents were asking the obvious questions about the expansion of our family. But this was one area where I felt the decision was up to Marilyn, since I would be away for half a year leaving her with the total responsibility and most of the work. Naturally, we talked about a family, debated the pros and cons, and usually ended up saying that we'd wait a little longer. In the back of both of our minds was the fact that our own life-style was diametrically opposed to the family life-styles in which both of us were raised. And that scared us a lot. Still in her mid-twenties, Marilyn wasn't in a race with the biological time clock yet.

Every aspect of my life—even family planning—was affected by football. I just couldn't make any long-range plans, since I never knew what would be the next step in my career. Who knew what fate would have in store for me in the upcoming season? That was the only way we could live: season by season.

During that summer, I thought a great deal about the possibility of leaving Buffalo. Feeling very ambivalent because I had grown to love the city and now had many friends there, I began fantasizing about being traded to another team. What I hated most about Buffalo was the climate. Going out on the field every day to practice or during home games, my hands would be so frozen that I'd never get the feel of the football. The icy weather was particularly tough on wide receivers because it's such a bitch to run on frozen ground, let alone catch the ball while wearing gloves. After a while, it would really get to me psychologically, and it had been particularly acute this past season, since I wasn't obsessed about my knee. I used to stand on the field all bundled up, wearing sweat shirts under my layers of jackets, with tape over the holes in my helmet which kept the wind out. I would daydream about the receivers in California running around in the sun.

Tony Greene flew out to LA that summer to spend a week with us. We had become inseparable friends, as well as roommates on the road, and I was glad that he was playing so well, since I seemed to have acquired the habit of befriending guys who would get cut. Tony and I discussed how different we both would become during the off-seasons. We would detach ourselves and become relatively normal. It dawned on me why the preseason games were so important to me. Being a five-year veteran, I would play as little as possible in the first few, and then as much as I could in the last two, because I needed to get used to being hit again. During the off-season, I would forget what it was like getting hit and having high-speed collisions. During even the shortest interval, my mind would repress that crunching, stomach-turning feeling of having another body smash into you at about 40 miles per hour. The preseason games woke me up in the same way that an armed-forces reservist is reawakened in boot camp before going on active duty.

Physically, I felt better than I had in a long time, and since Marilyn was so busy teaching and supervising the building of our pool, I decided to drive back to Buffalo a couple of weeks earlier. Tony Greene and I had already mapped out a training program that we would do together to get us in shape for training camp.

I drove leisurely across the country with nothing more on my mind than the thought of enjoying Buffalo before the city was iced over. Little did I know then what was in store for me that fall.

6

Coach Knox Knocks the NFL's Most Underrated Player—The Last Years in Buffalo

Little Chan
Together we became one.
Touching, feeling; knowing
    the serenity of contentment.
Silence transcending through
    sound; creating a bond
Stronger than words.
Touching, feeling; creating
    a consequence of this oneness.
Beauty taking shape firming, growing,
    dependent, yet secure
in a world of seahorses
Touching, feeling, changes
    everpresent.
Growing, life pumping through life.
Seahorses becoming real, capable of
    survival.

Touching, feeling the product of this oneness.
Dependent, searching for identity
The outside world has now become
the playground.
Caring, apprehensive, can these three
become one again?

—BOB CHANDLER
1978—Buffalo, New York
Before Marisa's birth.

During my years playing for Buffalo, I was watching the evolution of pro football before my very eyes. With the passing seasons, the game became less and less football and more and more entertainment. I mean this in the sense that each team generated for its owners many millions of dollars from the networks. It seemed as if the public couldn't get enough of football, what with the Sunday games, Monday night football, occasional Thursday night games, and Saturday broadcasts. Consequently, the NFL players became television personalities, and we had to look the part. In the past season of 1975, the NFL set a new standard regarding dress codes on the playing field.

Your pants had to cover your knees. Socks had to be at the bottom of your pants. You had to put black tape on black shoes and never wear dark tape on white shoes. Your shirt had to be tucked in all the time. You were required to wear knee pads, thigh pads, and hip pads. I was amazed they didn't require groin pads and belly pads. I personally felt that there was no justification for these dress codes other than making sure that all of us looked "uniform" on television. The NFL admitted that they just didn't want a bunch of rag-tag, sloppy-looking guys running around on the field out there. After all, they reasoned, what would our viewers think? Actually, the TV football fan who was relaxing in his shorts, torn T-shirt and bare feet while guzzling a few beers would probably feel more comfortable if the players didn't look like a bunch of cadets.

There had to be some wise guy somewhere along the line who convinced the NFL that TV ratings would increase if only the players looked tidier. The league actually assigned a guy who would be stationed on the sidelines of every game holding a clipboard with the rosters of players. And suddenly players were being fined for using the wrong kind of tape or committing the unspeakable crime of not pulling your socks up. I was fined four weeks in a row because the white socks that I wore over my striped red, white and blue socks were pulled so high that not enough blue showed up on the television screen. The fines started at $100 and generally escalated for those who were incorrigible like myself. I remember reading at that time about Fred Belitnikoff, who was playing for the Oakland Raiders. He just couldn't stand to have his pants pulled over his knees; also, he would cut his jersey sleeves so that they were billowy and hung loose. The NFL watchdog fined him every week, and the story goes that the Raiders' owner, Al Davis, paid a large sum of money just on Fred's uniform fines alone. Davis was smart enough to just pay the fines himself instead of trying to get Fred to clean up his act. Al knew that the way Fred dressed was part of his mental preparedness and the feel that he needed to perform.

I was so pissed off about these regulations that I wrote a letter to Pete Rozelle. I stated that if I was getting the shit kicked out of me during the games, I didn't need to have someone tell me how to dress for them. I went on to say that I couldn't comprehend how some guys who never had to put their asses on the line could be so petty about something as insignificant as dress codes. As long as you showed up in the right uniform, how you wore your socks and what pads you chose to cover yourself with should be your own business. After writing the letter, I never mailed it, but I later wished I had, if only to find out how Rozelle would have reacted.

The game had evolved in another negative way for me. When I first started in the pros, the good players played very hard and respected the good players on the opposing teams. They played a rough, tough, physical kind of football, but simultaneously they took care of each other. For example, if a guy was going out of bounds, these players wouldn't take a cheap shot at him which could cause serious physical damage. The empathy between players was incredible, because they all knew what the other guy would go through if he got hurt. And being responsible for a career-ending injury was not something to be proud of.

The game changed when the competition to play professional football became more intense. So much more money was being thrown around and individual players had the terrible pressure of whether or not they were going to make it. So these players started doing things that they hadn't normally done. As the equipment got better, many guys started using their head as a battering ram because the helmets were so failproof. Slowly, the feeling surfaced with players no longer respecting the other man's well-being on the opposing team. Each succeeding week, I would see more guys taking more and more cheap shots. It was as if these guys seemed to derive pride or some kind of pleasure by knocking a player out. When a player was sprawled in the dirt or lying on the ground gasping for breath, the opposing players would come over to him and taunt him about his injury. Now when a player was going out of bounds or was held up, and it was evident that he wasn't going anywhere, opposing players would come in for the kill.

I recall a couple of guys we often played against in Miami, Dick Anderson and Tim Foley. Both were defensive backs. These guys would knock the shit out of you, but they were always fair about it. I mean, many a time they'd hit you so hard you couldn't see straight, but I always respected them since I knew they just played a tough, physical game. And I never had the fear that they'd break my neck because of a cheap shot or that I'd sustain a knee injury because they hit me low when I wasn't expecting it.

Throughout professional football, the incidence of knee injuries and upper-body injuries such as shoulder separations and concussions was increasing. It wasn't totally the players' fault.

We were playing on more artificial surfaces, which was a horrendous problem in itself. Artificial surfaces were the answer to the network people's fervent prayers; they present the perfect background for television, since the field is in good shape all the time. It's also ideal for the owners because of low maintenance costs. At first, the players were successful in getting certain kinds of artificial turf eliminated because it was so dangerous. Then more expensive types started coming in, and because of management's large investment, we found that our collective voices against artificial turf were not being heard. Most of the NFL players favored real grass, which has so much more give to it. And if we couldn't get it in the stadiums, then we wanted it for our practice fields. Management never got its priorities straight, since there rarely seemed to be concern for the well-being of the players.

The artificial turf in Buffalo was not without its problems, either. It was one of the better-cushioned surfaces in the league, but it was so severely crowned for drainage that it created a very hazardous condition for knees and ankles. (Crowning a field means the center part is much higher than the sidelines.) Rich Stadium's crown was about 18 inches, so if you stood on one sideline and looked across the field, you couldn't see the other team's feet. Running on this kind of an angle every day eventually takes its toll.

Our new shoes were also culprits, and we were issued a different pair for every kind of surface. These shoes are designed for maximum traction, and on artificial turf, there is absolutely no give, which wears the hell out of your joints while causing some wicked foot injuries. Additionally, the increased velocity of the game made the players feel so much freer to throw their bodies around with little regard for the consequences.

Given all these drawbacks, I was still anticipating the season of 1976. I guess I was always optimistic whenever I was physically together. I spent a week in Buffalo staying at Tony Greene's apartment while Tony and I played racquetball daily. As training camp began, I was at long last looking forward to the competition among Hill, Rashad, and me. But nothing like that ever took place.

When Ahmad was injured last season, he was in the option year of his contract. It meant that he was free to talk to any team in the league and sign with them without compensation. This was before the new contract with its compensation clause came into being. All the Bills had to do was meet the other team's offer to keep him. But Buffalo lost Rashad to Seattle over what was rumored to be a mere $5,000 more than the Bills were willing to pay. Rashad had too much pride, and if Buffalo didn't want to match the offer, he would, and did, reluctantly leave. Buffalo lost probably the finest receiver in the game, and actually got nothing in return.

I was incredibly disappointed about the loss of Rashad. He was such a classy guy and added so much to the team. Our team was special because of guys like him and O.J. From then on, I looked at Buffalo's management through different eyes.

During the past season, Buffalo set an NFL attendance record, and we seemed to be at the point where either we were going to become a great team or we would begin to start going downhill. For me, the first step in going backward was losing Rashad. The effect on the team's morale was unreal. O. J. Simpson had become one of Ahmad's closest buddies, and O.J. was devastated when they failed to sign him.

Training camp contained some other surprises that season. O. J. Simpson never showed up because he was holding out for a bigger contract. Lou Saban was doing his best without Rashad and O.J. Saban begged Ralph Wilson, the Bills owner, not to capitulate by signing O.J. as it would open up the floodgates for all the other players' demands for bigger contracts. Without notifying Saban, Wilson signed O.J. to an $800,000-a-year contract. At that time it was the biggest contract that had ever been paid to a professional football player. Now, you've got to put all of this in perspective, since no one else on the team was making much over $100,000. Nobody resented O.J. for getting that sum, but looking at their own situation, the other players, including myself, felt like we were grossly underpaid.

The game has gone through a tremendous evolution over the last decade. It's gone from a sport to an entertainment. The obvious benefits to the players are higher salaries because of the added exposure and television contracts. The drawback is that there was an innocence that was stripped away from the game itself and the players. Football has become big business, and if you don't adjust, you fall by the wayside. Take, for example, the salary structure. In 1971, I got a $13,500 bonus and a three year contract of $15,000, $17,500, and $20,000. Today, someone in a similar position would expect to receive a $100,000 + bonus and salaries of $75,000, $100,000, and $125,000. It would be much more if the player was a high draft choice. Naturally, the players have assumed the identity of quasi-businessmen and are aware of the fact that they should be carrying briefcases, even if they're empty.

The public has an unrealistic view of players and their wealth. Football, although changing dramatically, is not in the same ballpark as baseball or basketball. Your average career is five years with an average annual salary of $100,000. Obviously, this won't set a player for life. Usually, the player adjusts his life-style according to what he makes each year and lacks the motivation to save much money. Thus, when a career ends abruptly—and most of them do—the player has very little to show for what he has done except for a few bodily scars. The result is an uneducated, twenty-seven-year-old football player with virtually no experience in the working world and very little idea of where to start!

Jim Braxton, our other fullback, said he wasn't going to play unless he got a raise. After much cajoling, he did play, but his heart wasn't in it, and his playing was decidedly lackluster. Braxton was incredible. The 250-pound fullback from Virginia, who came in with me in 1971, had become a good friend. Braxton didn't block people; he ran over them. His biggest booster was O.J. who totally understood Jim's value to him as a runner. Besides being one of the leaders on the team, Jim was also the smartest player on the field. On many occasions when things became hectic and nobody on the team could hear themselves think through the deafening roar of the crowd, Braxton would be directing everyone to where they should go—even O.J. He was like having a coach out on the playing field with you.

Lou Saban was having problems other than the team's morale. His wife had become very depressed, and in the middle of the season, she was found dead. Understandably, Lou never recovered from that. Everything in his life was beginning to crumble at that time. The great organization which contained "The Electric Company" was falling apart. I'll never forget his telling us in early October that he could no longer do the job that was necessary, and for the good of the team, he believed it was time for him to step down and go elsewhere. I was absolutely crushed. I had never had so much respect for anyone, whether coach, teacher or friend, as I had for Lou Saban. He was the one man who really made the difference in my career. Lou's leaving Buffalo cast a real gloom over that season.

Ralph Wilson then upgraded our offensive line coach, Jim Ringo, to head coach. Jim had masterminded and engineered The Electric Company and was probably *the* best offensive line coach in the game. But he was soon to learn that there's an enormous difference between being offensive line coach and head coach. Ringo had learned his football from Vince Lombardi as a center for the Green Bay Packers. Jim was from the old school of football; he was many times All-Pro and later elected into the Football Hall of Fame.

Jim Ringo was a competitive, compassionate, caring man. He believed that playing the game was a privilege—not a right. But at this point, the game had passed him by. Professional football players had changed and Ringo hadn't. When he had played the game, he gave it everything he had every single week. More importantly, he held a reverence for the game. He couldn't understand why talented athletes didn't love this game the way he had. And why so many wouldn't put out more than 75 percent of themselves on the field. Ringo deserved the head coaching job. But his inability to cope with this new breed of player—these guys that had to be coaxed and babied to perform their job—was his eventual undoing.

Everything that Lou Saban had built soon eroded. Some of our players were destroying our team and its chances simply because they no longer cared. There were about twelve players that Ringo knew really cared, and I was among them. He would always try to reassure us by saying, "We're gonna make this thing right, guys. Soon, I'll get the kind of players that I need in here, so just hang in with me till then."

But we were outnumbered by the players who didn't give a damn. Most of the bellyaching centered around those who felt they were underpaid. Now this doesn't exist on every team, but it always seemed to be a problem in Buffalo. It probably stemmed from the fact that management justified what they were paying you by degrading your abilities. This tactic made most players feel not only that they were underpaid but also that their playing ability was suspect.

I'll never forget the day Tony Greene went in to the front office to negotiate a new contract. He was reportedly told by the Bills' general manager that "on a scale of one to ten, you're at best a seven, and this is the salary we would pay a seven." This was said to Tony in spite of the fact that he was All-Pro as well as the man Bob Griese claimed was the toughest to throw against in the entire NFL. Unfortunately, playing football is like any other business; when a player feels that the organization doesn't appreciate him, it's likely that he'll never give that little extra something which could turn the team into a winner. You see, a team's strength starts at the top, works down through the management, the coaches and then the players. If any of these aspects doesn't work as a cohesive and quality unit, a team will not maintain a winning edge. So when this kind of materialistic discontent sets in, it's damn near impossible to turn it around. Economics were economics, and malcontents became bigger malcontents.

Another memorable moment was an early morning meeting Ringo called toward the end of the season. Very slowly and quietly he began talking, and in the manner of Lou Saban, he kept getting madder and madder until it really looked like he was going to burst a blood vessel. As angry as he had become, I found it difficult to keep from laughing because of the subject matter. He was saying, "All you guys think about are your fucking three-hundred-dollar alligator shoes and your fucking eight-hundred-dollar suits. And then you pull up here in your goddamn Mercedes and Jaguars." Poor Ringo was making an emotional plea for the players to get their shit together, forget about all of their material rewards, and start playing football again. This was a serious matter to him and it went on for about an hour.

I'll never forget walking out of that meeting and going into the training room, to make a phone call. On the other phone was Sherman White, a defensive end, who was phoning someone in California where he lived. He was placing an order for a fifty-thousand-dollar Mercedes 450 SLC, and this within five minutes of Ringo's heart-wrenching speech.

It was amazing how psychological attitudes of the players could demolish a team's record. Ringo started loathing a defensive back, Dwight Harrison, who wouldn't want to play if anything at all bothered him. Now, Harrison was potentially a great player, but he evidently wanted to get traded to another team, and he was not particularly cooperative for Ringo either. After one of our last games, I had left my shaving kit in the locker room and returned after everyone had gone. As I got my bag, I heard someone talking where there was a light on over at the other end of the locker room. I walked over quietly, and from behind a row of lockers, I saw Ringo wearing a pair of red sweat pants and a gray T-shirt. He had one sock on and one foot was barefoot, and one leg of his sweat pants was rolled up. Smoking a cigarette, he was standing in front of Dwight Harrison's locker talking to Dwight's nameplate. He muttered, "Harrison, you son of a bitch, I'll get you. One of these days I'll get you!" I sneaked out of the locker room as quietly as I could because it was painful for me to see such a proud man at the end of his rope.

I felt sorry for Ringo, but it would have happened to anyone who took Lou's place, since Saban would be the first to admit that the ship had already started to sink. The Bills' record for that season was two and twelve. Buffalo still led the NFL in attendance, and I thought that the fans were filling the stadium out of disbelief that their team could turn for the worst so fast. It's funny how quickly you accept being a loser again. We had had a brief moment of a few years' glory when we were a top-notch team, then suddenly, you're stunned, you're shocked, but you're a loser again.

This loser stigma haunted me by the end of the season. I caught sixty-one passes for ten TDs that year, many when the game was gone, which you're usually not given as much credit for. What nobody realizes is that those passes are as difficult to catch when you're losing as when you're winning. This type of thinking must have tainted the voting for the Pro Bowl, since I was the leading receiver in the AFC but once again didn't get invited to this postseason game.

By the time I reached California for Christmas, I felt my disillusionment setting in. I mean, it was ridiculous what I had put myself through. Every Saturday night, my elbows would be the size of golf balls and need to be drained before the next day's game. I'd finish every game and I couldn't even bend my arms. They'd be wrapped tight, and then a few cc's of Xylocaine would be administered to calm down the bursal sac in the elbow joints. I caught a lot of my passes on the sidelines, and when you have to make sure your feet are in bounds, you generally fall with your elbows hitting the ground first. I started taking six aspirins a day throughout the entire season to help quiet things down in my body.

The fact that I had been slighted by the Pro Bowl only served to motivate me even more. I worked my ass off during that offseason in order to convince myself that I was one of the best in the sport. I just had to do a little more and try again next year.

Coach Ringo phoned me during the off-season saying that we were going to get everything together back here, start off on the right foot and get this loser image turned around. He believed it, and I wanted to believe him.

In mid-March Marilyn and I flew back to Washington, D.C., for an NFL Players Association awards banquet. At this really nifty black-tie dinner, I was given a magnificent plaque engraved with my name, number, number of receptions, and yardage gained. I was still bitter about not making the All-Pro team, but this banquet and what it stood for was very special to me. Marilyn and I had a fantastic time in the nation's capital, and for the first time, she was able to enjoy the recognition I received. On this night she could almost understand that football was worth it despite the six-month separations and my various injuries.

Flying home together, Marilyn mused aloud that she was getting tired of teaching and was thinking of coming back with me to Buffalo to try being together year-round for a change. I was scared out of my mind, thinking that my entire routine would be shot. I really craved that freedom of no time schedules and being able to go out with the guys at night. I wasn't playing around, but freedom to do as I pleased had become a way of life for me now. I loved being the "married bachelor," which made everyone very jealous. I had had six years of doing it my way, and I was put off by the thought of coming home and having responsibilities after practice. Marilyn bought the fact that I wanted her in California, working and taking care of the house. However, I'm still not completely sure that she believed it as much as I wanted her to.

My wife is pretty much of a loner, feeling the need for just a few close friends to share with. But for the most part, during the times I was gone, she would spend a lot of time with her dad, who is really one of her best friends. Twice a week, he would come up to have dinner with her, and every Saturday morning, he'd be over to help with the gardening and take her out to breakfast. She swam every day to stay in shape, taught, and waited for her phone calls every night from me. I would call her at midnight my time, which was 9:00 P.M. in California. Sometimes there'd be music in the bar I was calling from, which led Marilyn to wonder where the hell I was and why wasn't I getting more sleep. I would usually reply that I got enough sleep after practice, which I did.

Deciding to leave my Porsche at home, I flew back to our training camp at Niagara University and made the decision to get an apartment in town. Tony Greene helped me find a building that had real character, with leaded glass windows and hardwood floors—800 West Ferry. It was a beauty. It was so charming that Marilyn flew back three times that year just to help me decorate the place. I had the luxury of driving a white Corvette that I had gotten from Hunt Chevrolet in Buffalo in exchange for appearing four times a year to sign autographs and provide some tickets for the game.

The season of 1977 was very shaky for the Buffalo Bills. By the fourth game, O.J. had broken his foot and missed a number of games. Then, he tore his knee and had to fly to the west coast for surgery. He flew back to Buffalo a few times, only to watch games from the bench. Then our quarterback, Joe Ferguson, got hurt and was out for seven games. The backup quarterback, Gary Marangi, would ordinarily play wonderfully coming in as a second-stringer, but as a starter, he had a real shaky time. Gary developed a shoulder problem that changed his entire throwing motion. No one could diagnose the problem, so they made him feel that it was *all* mental. He became so uptight that he reached the point where he couldn't throw a spiral pass anymore. Imagine a guy who could hit bull's-eyes with darts at sixty yards, not being able to throw the football at all. He even went to several hypnotists, but his passing didn't improve much. Marangi, one of the brightest prospects in professional football, was never able to correct his shoulder problem and overcome the mental anguish of having lost his valuable skills so quickly. After he completed this disastrous season, Gary Marangi, like so many of my close football colleagues, became a memory. Despite everything, I managed to grab sixty balls while the team ingloriously chalked up three wins in fourteen games. So, needless to say, there weren't a whole lot of game-winning catches.

The attendance at Rich Stadium dwindled down to 30,000. The people in Buffalo were angry and disappointed.

Tony and I would go out at night and could feel the hostility again from the fans. It made me angry because Tony and I were busting our asses and were among the few bright spots on the team. Whereas before I used to look forward to seeing all the people at the bars and restaurants, now I felt a real distaste for everyone who spoke to us. It became tiresome to keep hearing remarks about how awful the Buffalo Bills had become. At the beginning of the season, I would take time to explain to these people some fine points about a game or some players. By November, I had had it with people who'd always start their sermons with, "I hate to bother you, but . . ." Again, the fans felt that they owned us, paid our salaries, and had every right to berate us whenever they felt like it. I no longer liked being recognized as a football player in this adopted city of mine.

The one thing that cheered me during that depressing year was the fact that Marilyn was expecting our first baby. Having become disillusioned with teaching in the public schools, she was ready for a new direction. The two of us had come a long way in our marriage, and we were feeling secure enough to enlarge our own family. Now that I was less than excited about my profession of football, it seemed kind of natural for me to be anticipating a new profession—fatherhood.

The biggest problem for Marilyn was being alone while pregnant. Thank God she had an uncomplicated pregnancy and felt pretty well through the long hard months. She wasn't showing when I left for training camp in July, so naturally I got a kick out of seeing the photos she sent me when her stomach began to bulge. It seemed unreal in the sense that my absence made me feel like a father-by-proxy. I mean, I knew I was soon to be a first-time father, but being away for so many months sometimes made me feel that Marilyn was becoming a mother while I would soon be an uncle or some other once-removed relative.

The baby was due on November 29, and believe me, I still marvel how doctors think they can predict the day of birth. The trouble is that they're seldom right. Fate was smiling in that we were playing the Oakland Raiders on November 28. I caught nine passes and had one of the better games of my career, even though the Bills lost. Ringo gave me permission to fly down to LA that night so I could go with Marilyn to the hospital the next day. It was wonderful seeing Marilyn after four months, and it was as if all the expectancy hit me at once. The next day our kid didn't seem to be anxious to see the light of day, which made us realize that you can't push Mother Nature. By Wednesday, November 30, I was getting antsy because I knew I should have been back in Buffalo practicing for the Redskins game on Sunday. I wasn't going to get fired for not being in Buffalo, but I felt I was overstepping a privilege Ringo had given me. I've never liked abusing the goodwill of others, and yet, in retrospect, I should have stayed. Marilyn's obstetrician was willing to try to induce labor, but since this was a first child, it still could take a very long time. I was truly betwixt and between until Marilyn convinced me to go back. She knew what tremendous pressure they put on you to be at practice. So I caught a midnight flight to Chicago with the hope of connecting and being in Buffalo the following morning for Thursday practice.

Then I became violently sick while waiting for my connection at O'Hare Airport. Imagine me almost missing my flight because I couldn't stop throwing up in the airport's john. By the time I got to my apartment the following morning in a howling blizzard in Buffalo, I had to phone Bud Tice, one of the trainers, to explain that I had the flu and wouldn't be able to make it in to practice. That night, Tony Greene brought over hot chicken soup and juices, which we agreed would cure anything. The next day I was still feeling lousy, but managed to go through the motions at practice. While on the field, I was told that Marilyn had just gone into labor. I phoned the hospital immediately and was told that everything was okay and that my sister Cathy was going to be her coach in the delivery room. I went completely crazy worrying about Marilyn and wondering if I'd made the right decision in returning to Buffalo.

I was in bed at 9:00 P.M. when I got the news that our daughter Marisa had just arrived. Happy that mother and child were doing fine, I still felt lots of regret not being with them. I could always rationalize that I would've come down with the flu in LA, which would've kept me out of the delivery room, but I suspected that I was just mollifying myself.

Tony and Jim Braxton dragged me out of my sickbed that evening to celebrate the newest Chandler, and by the second bottle of champagne, I no longer had the flu, or at least was put out of my misery.

Although Marilyn had gotten along beautifully in the delivery room and sounded so happy when she called me Friday night, she felt terrible the following day and was disappointed that I wasn't with her at this momentous time of our lives. Football seemed to be a convenient excuse for all the responsibilities at home I wanted to dodge.

Our only consolation came on Sunday when the million-dollar scoreboard at Rich Stadium blared out the following message for local and network viewers alike: "Congratulations Bob and Marilyn Chandler on your daughter, Marisa Louise, born last Friday!" Three weeks later, I began enjoying the responsibilities of fatherhood when my two girls met me at the LA airport. In fact, during the entire off-season, I would look forward to studying my law books while rocking Marisa to sleep.

The only unsettling thing for me that spring and early summer was anticipating a new head coach, who was due to take the reins at training camp.

Optimism runs rampant.
New faces, anticipating great success.
    The molding of a team.
    Getting to know each other.
    Learning what's expected.
A fresh start.
Erasing shadows of doubt.
    How good are we?
Hours of sweat and study give way to performance.
Hustle and enthusiasm mask deficiencies.
    Struggling, fighting, but falling short.
    Maybe we're not that good.

Don't say it's true, too many illusions have already
    been endured.
But yes, again success eludes us.
    Reality, disguised as a cold November wind,
    bears truth on our plight.
Expectations have vanished.
Time is once again our companion.
    Pride endures December.
    Snowfall brings signs of future strength.
Optimism rekindled.
    Next year will be our year,
    Or so they say!

—BOB CHANDLER
1978—Los Angeles, California
Before the first training
camp with Chuck Knox.

Chuck Knox really came to Buffalo trailing clouds of glory. He was the champion of champions, having just spent five years coaching the Los Angeles Rams and taking them to five division championships! Five, count 'em, five. Like Sleeping Beauty waiting for Prince Charming, the city of Buffalo awaited Coach Knox. By the fall of 1978, the fans of the Buffalo Bills had gone through periods of frenzied happiness as well as deadly bitterness.

The city itself was going through gyrations as many big corporate headquarters moved away while giant Bethlehem Steel was slowly shutting down. The city's basketball team was getting ready to leave, and although hockey was big, the team was made up of mostly Canadian players. It was football for which the city was saving its heart and soul. It had come down to the point that when the Bills won, it felt like the entire city of Buffalo won. And if we got beat by, for example, Cleveland, Chicago, or Pittsburgh, then the city's population would feel dishonored, as if those winning cities were better places in which to live.

From his exposure in Hollywood, Chuck Knox was no stran-

Two years old, with my grandmother in Long Beach, California.

Five years old, Long Beach, California.
Photo by Glenn Mark Studio.

Choir boy, St. Luke's Episcopal Church, Long Beach, California.

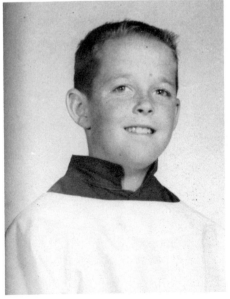

Quarterback, Whittier High School, Whittier, California, 1966.

My high school graduation picture,
Whittier High School, 1967.
Photo by Cummings-Prentiss Studio.

My "perm look," for an ad that ran in *Buffalo Magazine* in 1975.
Photo by P. Souto, Crescent.

Rich Stadium, Buffalo, 1977:
"I couldn't believe I dropped it!"
Photo by Robert L. Smith "Photography."

Pre-game, 1980.
Photo courtesy of Los Angeles Raiders.

In action, 1980.
Photo courtesy of Los Angeles Raiders.

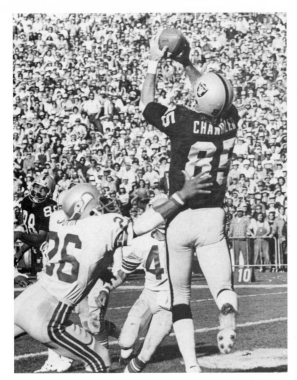

The first of three touchdown catches against Seattle at Oakland Coliseum, 1980.

Photo by Russ Reed.

The winning touchdown catch against Miami, also at Oakland, 1980.

Photo by Russ Reed.

My first catch of the 1981 Superbowl—the biggest game of
my career!

Photo courtesy of Los Angeles Raiders.

"Chandler hits the ground." (Superbowl '81)

Photo by Michael Zagaris (California Photo Service).

One week after our Superbowl victory, here I am in Hawaii in the
Superteams Competition versus Philadelphia.

Off-season Superbowl party,
Beverly Hilton, Los Angeles.
Photo by Norm Fisher,
California Photo Service.

Just before the 1982 season, the last few happy days before my right knee blew out and ended my career.

Photo © 1982 by Peter Read Miller.

Marilyn, Marisa, and I.

*Photo © 1982
by Peter Read Miller.*

ger to the tailored public relations campaign. No sooner had he arrived in Buffalo than he masterminded a plan to change the current negative attitude of the Bills' fans. Initiating the slogan "Talking Proud," he wanted to instill a new sense of pride in this sports-minded city. The campaign took off like a forest fire, and soon most adults were wearing lapel pins and badges that said, "Talking Proud." The kids from every grade level used the term as their war cry, and even the newspapers bandied the slogan around incessantly. Coach Knox had correctly assessed the city when he unleashed this tide of "group think." It almost spooked me. I remember phoning Marilyn and describing the situation as if Knox had been exerting mind control over the Buffalonians.

How could I ever forget my first encounter with this man. Training-camp practice at Niagara University ended at 5:00 P.M. After all these years of playing with the big boys, I was still staying out after practice to catch balls from anyone who'd throw them. Part of this extra effort stemmed from my own fear of failure, while some of it came from a high school mentality that wanted to show the coaches how lucky they were to have such a great player who was so dedicated and actually cared. By the time I got to the locker room, most of the guys were already dressed and on their way to dinner, which was held from 5:30 to 6:30.

Tony Greene grabbed me and said he needed a ride into Buffalo (twenty minutes away) to pick up his car. So I took a quick shower, skipped my treatment of ice on the knees and back, and was out of the door in ten minutes. We made a quick stop in the dining hall to check in with one of the go-fers (young ball boys hired by the team during training camp) who was checking off our names. All meals are mandatory at training camp, but we decided to forego our supper and soon we were speeding down Interstate 90 along the Niagara River to Buffalo at about 80 miles per hour. (We usually drove a "bit" over the speed limit, knowing that the "talking proud" patrolmen would never ticket two Buffalo Bills.) I dropped Tony off and immediately sped back to Niagara University to see if I could pick up a quick salad and some ice cream before the seven o'clock meeting.

The dining hall was below ground level and there were two different ways to enter. Since we had a check-in procedure, one door was designated as the entrance and the other as an exit. I happened to pull my car up next to the exit door, and since it was 6:45, I entered through it, thinking that everyone would be gone. As I ran through the door, I came upon Bud Thalmann, the PR director, and his assistant, Mike Shaw, and Coach Knox. Startled, I said hello and headed toward the salad bar. As I was filling my plate, Knox came up behind me saying, "Where have you been, and why are you so late?"

His aggravated attitude immediately put me on the defensive, and therefore my response was less than polite. I said, "I was here at five forty-five and checked in with your boy outside and then left to run an errand. I'm here now to grab a salad before the meeting—is that all right?"

Knox furrowed his brow, saying, "Dinner is between five-thirty and six-thirty! And that isn't my boy out there!"

"Okay, I'm sorry," I replied. "I was in a rush."

He said, "Don't worry about it. I just wanted to be sure that we're going to be on the same page." Expressionless, he stopped and glared at me, and then he said as an afterthought, "By the way, that's the exit, not the entrance." On that sour note, I just set my tray down on the nearest table and made sure that I walked out the door marked "entrance." Even though I knew that I acted like a spoiled child, I had a gut feeling that no matter how hard I tried, Knox and I would always be like oil and water.

I later learned from Mike Shaw that Knox had said, "I guess I showed that little son of a bitch," after I left the dining hall. I immediately thought of Lou Saban, who gave respect and got it back in spades. Mike went on to say that ever since that first meeting, Chuck Knox never had very many nice things to say about me. Jesus, I'd been busting my ass for a lot of years on this team, and now the new man in charge was making a summary judgment based on personality and not performance. The fascinating part was that Knox was always polite to me off the field, and sometimes he almost seemed cordial.

During the training camp my knee started bothering me again with a sore lump on the outside, and it actually made a clicking sound every time I would bend it. At first, Dr. Godfrey wanted to send me to a special clinic in Toronto for arthroscopic surgery, but he later reconsidered and wanted me to be treated in Buffalo. They took a bundle of x-rays of the knee, and by this time I was getting a little paranoid about x-rays, since I had had so many that I thought I could glow in the dark from the radiation.

When Godfrey advised going in and opening up the knee, I agreed, on the condition that I didn't have to undergo general anesthesia. Anesthesia had always frightened me, and I figured I'd had enough to last me a few lifetimes. Godfrey operated on me at Mercy Hospital in South Buffalo; after about a dozen injections of a pain-killing drug, and a tourniquet to block circulation, my knee was opened up. Being awake with a little tent pulled around my face, I could hear and feel Dr. Godfrey grinding away. He pulled out a mass of tissue that had accumulated around a stitch in the knee capsule which hadn't dissolved from my last surgery.

Part of my recuperative therapy was having Marilyn and Marisa come out to visit. My wife was particularly concerned, since this was my fourth knee operation. Learning from my past history of being impatient, I did wait until the incision healed before I was ready to play, which was still only four weeks later.

I was particularly anxious to begin playing during that 1978 season just to see how my knee would react under stress. And while my knee was coming back, I thought I'd start by playing some racquetball. But everything was changed by Coach Knox. The entire team was prohibited from playing basketball and racquetball because a player had sprained his ankle going in for a layup in a pickup game and couldn't play the following Sunday. The loss of racquetball really stung me hard. I believed we were responsible adults who could take care of ourselves in most activities off the field. I truly felt I needed that activity to keep me in shape; plus it was important for me to retain my quickness along with my hand and eye coordination.

Knox also precluded our laying around in the training room before practice. Some of the veterans used to enjoy coming in, getting their cup of coffee, laying down on the training tables and bullshitting with Eddie (Abe) Abramowski and Bud Tice, the trainers. A few of us would even grab a wink or two.

I'll admit that I was one of the more vociferous team members regarding the Knox innovations, but what the hell, I'd been there a long time, was getting kind of crotchety and extremely resistant to change.

The one thing we managed to retain was a locker room gag that we pulled on the rookies every Thanksgiving. We'd pass out flyers two days before Thanksgiving that said all players were entitled to a twenty-pound turkey at a specified grocery store free of charge. Just sign up and show up. It was indicated that the store owner was a dyed-in-the-wool Bills' fan, and this was the only way he could show his appreciation for his team. Directions for getting to the store were furnished at the bottom of the flyers.

We would hide a couple of guys down at the store to verify what happened. Now, remember that the store people knew absolutely nothing about this gag. Try to picture a 290-pound defensive lineman who's told his wife not to buy a turkey because he was getting one free showing up at this store and asking the manager for his turkey. Some of the guys got pretty huffy about it and often would demand a free turkey. It was such a ball watching the poor store manager trying to tell these giants that they'd been had. The best part came the following morning at practice when those guys came in and tried to pretend that they never fell for the gag—until our eyewitnesses refreshed their memories.

Knox was so determined to turn our team around that he damn near willed it. Talk about talking proud! We weren't winning every game, but we had become very competitive. Knox and his people made some fine draft choices that season, and for the first time in two years, we actually had a defense that worked. From Pittsburgh, they acquired a wide receiver, Frank Lewis, who'd had a multifaceted career peppered with many injuries. He was a helluva lot smarter than me in that he took excellent care of himself. He didn't go out at night, was in bed early, and would definitely not go to practice if something was bothering him. Buffalo literally stole Frank from a Pittsburgh team that thought his playing days were over.

Knox admitted he'd need a couple of years to shape the Bills into the team he ultimately wanted. He really had a knack for motivating us to feel like a bunch of hit men, and the players ate this up. We began to feel like the bad guys, whose motto was: "Whoever plays the Bills may win, but they're going to get the hell kicked out of them first." That's what "Bills" football was all about.

Around this time, someone from radio station WKBW approached me about the possibility of doing a radio show. This was the local station that broadcast all the Bills' games, and since I had done many radio and TV interviews over the past three seasons, they seemed to think I'd be a good spokesman for three five-minute shows a week at seven in the morning. Evidently, their marketing research found me to be fairly popular with the fans. (I figured they probably did their market research in some of the bars and restaurants we frequented every evening.)

Knox had a radio show in the evenings on a competitive station, and he also had a weekly television show where he performed with incredible poise. Naturally, I asked him if he would mind my having three spots a week on the radio. Knowing that he wasn't crazy about my doing this, I soft-pedaled the show as being a namby-pamby postgame, pregame, and what-was-happening-during-the-week type of program. Begrudgingly, he said okay, with the warning to be careful about what I said.

The show was a riot, as the station would phone me a few minutes before air time to awaken me and let me sit up and talk to myself to get the mental wheels spinning. Half the time I couldn't remember what the hell I said, since I was usually in a state of semiconsciousness. I did this show for two years, and it wasn't until the second year that I suspected Knox had someone occasionally record or listen to some of my programs to check on the content. He approached me a number of times during each season and would comment about certain things I had said on the air. It gave him another reason for disliking me. Interestingly, none of my teammates resented my having the show. They loved it. They would listen religiously and usually give me a hard time when I didn't mention certain guys who felt they deserved more attention.

With the radio show doing well, I was becoming kind of special in Buffalo. Having done a hair salon ad exhorting men to get their hair curled, I was approached by the printer of *Buffalo* magazine, which was running the ad. He wanted me to pose for a poster which hopefully people would buy for three dollars each. Since I was a closet ham, I thought this would be a great idea, especially since I could pose in a Levi shirt and jeans. So we did it.

I went out to the large shopping malls and autographed the poster, and within a few weeks, the printer sold his entire stock of thirty-five hundred. I gotta confess that I was embarrassed signing this so-called sexy reproduction of myself, but it was a flattering experience. Guess what? Knox wasn't crazy about my doing the poster. But he was never overt about it, either. He made a few snide remarks about it and the fact that I was still having my hair curled.

Despite all of these extracurricular activities, I was trying to gear up for a good year. Because of my newly cut knee, I had to miss the first four games. However, by the end of the season, I had caught forty-four passes, which made me feel good about myself. And that was considering the fact that I was playing at only 70 percent of my capacity.

In my first game back, we were playing Kansas City at Rich Stadium. I was lined up against a rookie defensive back, Gary Greene. Gary was a first-round draft choice who was very fast. The easiest guys to use a lot of fakes against are quick defensive backs because they always react to your fake. Players who aren't as quick on their feet have a tendency to get in your way, so you end up running pretty basic routes against them. I was able to throw a few veteran moves at Greene to see how he reacted. Countering my first fakes, Greene enabled me to catch seven passes for two touchdowns in my debut game for Coach Knox.

Cumulatively, I had caught 220 passes over the past four seasons, which was more than any other wide receiver in the NFL. As happy as I was with my own performance, I was witnessing things that season that spoiled what should have been a proud time for me.

Knox brought in a kicker named Tom Dempsey, who, with a clubfoot, had set the NFL record for the longest field goal of 63 yards. Tom was a heavy set guy who was always chewing tobacco on the field and was one of the nicest guys I'd ever met. He had a deformed hand and arm which looked like a little stub with pointers sticking from it. Despite these birth defects, Tom had a special shoe made for him to compensate for his having hardly any foot, and he would continually lift weights with this tiny arm. I was the man who held the football that he kicked for field goals and extra points. Since we would spend lots of time kicking after practice, I got to know him very well.

Our season was about two-thirds over, and I was out with Tony Greene and Lou Piccone at a place called Mother's, where we were having a few beers. Tom Dempsey came in looking shell-shocked and said, "Guys, I've just been released from the team."

"You're kidding," Tony said with a smile, not realizing that the final bell had indeed just tolled for Tom.

"It's because I missed that goddamned field goal. You know, the one that would've won the game for us."

Lou, Tony and I tried to bolster Dempsey's spirits, but nothing we could say helped as much as the many beers he consumed. He kept getting louder and more belligerent, which I figured was a good way of getting the hurting out of his system. When we finally convinced Tom to leave the bar, he walked out on the street with us, and suddenly, he just broke down, sobbing hysterically. I must confess that I always get very uptight watching someone become so emotional, and on that night, I didn't know what to say to him that would ease his pain. Finally, I said, "Tom, you still have that restaurant of yours down in New Orleans. And it's doing great."

Tom cried, "It's not the goddamned money I'm losing from being axed that's killing me. It's because I'm letting down all the handicapped people in this country! I was their hero because I showed the world that a handicapped guy could be a top professional athlete."

I yelled at him, "You made those people proud of you for a lot of years!"

Tom replied with a low moan, "I screwed up, Bob. Now I'm a failure in their eyes—now they're gonna feel that we're all a bunch of hopeless gimps!"

We stayed with him for a long time, but after he left, I still felt uneasy not knowing what he might do to himself while in this state. I felt like shouting out, "Christ! This game isn't that goddamned important in the whole scheme of things. It's supposed to be a game, and yet these coaches are fucking with people's lives." So what if he missed a lousy 22-yard field goal? Why should a man's career and life be ruined because of one lousy kick? Change! That's the important word to coaches and owners. Once a player incurs the anger of one of the higher-ups, his playing days have changed permanently.

When the season of 1978 ended, I was more than aware of the fact that Chuck Knox and I were not a chummy twosome. On the other hand, he was always very complimentary toward me in newspaper and television interviews, maybe making him a more gracious person than I was.

That off-season was one in which I worked out constantly whenever I wasn't cracking the books at law school. One of my USC trainers, Gary Tuthill, was now the trainer for the Rams, and he let us use the Rams' camp facilities. So there I was, working and training with another team. I realized I had a lucky break to be there, since most NFL teams are very paranoid about an outsider being in their camp. Actually, I was benefiting the Rams' defensive backs, because they got to look at a different kind of receiver, one they didn't have to face all season long, since the Bills so rarely played the Rams.

My only real physical liability was my chronic back pain. I played some golf that summer, and by the time I would get to the fifteenth or sixteenth hole, I'd have to sit down and rest, as my back would start going into spasms. Despite the back pains, I knew that I had a few good years of football left in me. Thank God, I no longer concerned myself about getting cut or being released from my contract.

My own feelings about Knox were that he still appreciated and depended on my abilities as a player. I truly believed that the bottom line in the NFL was playing well and that any personality differences could be set aside.

Coming back to training camp in July for the 1979 season, Tony Greene was a little more skeptical about staying on the team. Although he was one of the team captains, Tony knew that Knox also wasn't wild about him, and he kept telling me that he felt he was going to be phased out. This actually wouldn't be so unusual. When a new coach of Knox's caliber comes in, there is sometimes a major housecleaning. By that, I mean that a coach has to surround himself with his kind of people. At the same time, he has to pump new blood and a new attitude into the team. A team that had been through as many ups and downs as Buffalo had forgotten how to win and what it takes to be a winner. Players that had been on this roller coaster through the seventies weren't as receptive to another new system and approach—consequently, it wouldn't be such a bad idea to get rid of them regardless of their ability.

Training camp began, and my left knee started swelling again. One of the trainers who had become a close friend, Bud Tice, told Knox that I should take about ten days and do nothing but build this leg up via weights, bicycling, jogging and sprinting rather than practicing. Thus, I began the season out of step with the rest of the team and curiously scrutinized by Chuck Knox.

No matter how good you are or what you've done for the team, it's important to evaluate the draft choices. If they take a receiver in the first round, for example, they say innocently, "Don't worry, it has nothing to do with you. We're just taking the best athletes." Usually, that's bullshit, and then you start getting paranoid. The first-round draft choice that year for the Bills was Jerry Butler, a wide receiver. When I got to camp, I saw him play, and he was exceptionally good. Although he was a rookie, Jerry was ready to start this season. And sure enough, the ten days that I took off to build up my leg was just the right amount of time for Jerry to get used to starting.

Knox would stare at me as I was doing my thing while the rest of the team suffered through two grueling practice sessions a day. He must've thought that I considered myself way above the system. The paradox was that he knew I was good and that I was anxious to get back, while at the same time he'd frown at me as if to say, "This prima donna thinks he's running the whole god-damn show." Knox also inferred from my attitude that I felt I didn't have to worry about playing preseason games and certainly didn't need all of this double-days bullshit.

My teammates would joke around with me and would ask how they could join the exclusive country club I was in, since my life seemed pampered compared to their workouts. But the guys respected me as the kind of player who they knew would give everything during a game.

I was contemplating having a terrific year. And everything bode well for me in that direction. I sublet a great downtown apartment from a girlfriend of Tony's who was going away to school; the place was very plush with a wood-paneled bedroom complete with antique brass bed.

I had also decided to upgrade my car status by ordering a navy blue Mercedes 450SL (which set me back around $31,000), which was to be delivered to me in Buffalo by mid-September.

It was raining on the morning that I first went back to normal practice. Knox let us go out in our helmets, sweats and shorts, and since our regular playing field was flooded, we went to an upper field that was rarely used. While running some pass plays against the defense, Ferguson threw a kind of line drive that was a little bit away from me. Instead of letting it go, as anyone in a normal frame of mind would do, I dove for it and made a great fingertip catch. As I caught it, I heard an ominous crunching sound when my shoulder hit the ground, and I rolled over. When I got up, I could see that my shoulder was pointed in the opposite direction. I didn't have to be a genius to realize that I had completely separated my shoulder. It hurt like hell for just a minute or two, and then it just went numb. It was a ridiculous fact of my life that I could never go easy on myself in practice or play. Now, we're not talking about some green rookie who's trying to make a great first impression. I was someone with enough years under my belt who should've let that ball bounce all the way down to the Love Canal. Needless to say, I was devastated.

While walking way out of my way to avoid the coaches, I saw Tice running toward me with a worried expression on his face. I yelled out, "Just forget it. I don't want to talk about it. Leave me alone, goddamnit!"

I was about fifty yards away from Knox as I walked toward the locker room. All of a sudden, I started screaming at him, "You fucking asshole! We shouldn't be out in this fucking rain anyway. We should be inside. You're stupid to let us out in this crap." I had to take it out on somebody, and even though it obviously wasn't his fault it seemed appropriate at the time.

A brilliant move on my part. Particularly since Knox and I had been discussing a renegotiation of my contract that season. I was supposed to make $110,000 that year and had one more year left which would be at $117,000. Comparatively, I was underpaid and should have been receiving about $160,000 minimum. But I was doing my own negotiating, and naively I thought that I had pushed them to their willing limit every time. Also, it didn't make sense to hold out for a great deal more by not showing up ready to go at training camp, especially after the team just drafted a first-round wide receiver. But Knox had made overtures that he'd pay for the guys who'd play hard for him. All of this was spinning in my head as I walked off the field that day. Had I blown my new contract? Maybe Knox was bullshitting me, and then again, maybe he wasn't.

I was so upset at myself for ruining my shoulder at this crucial time. At this point, I was sitting on a table in the training room, and my whole life started to flash before my eyes. I thought of Marisa and Marilyn and thought about being home with them doing anything but playing football. I was convinced that football was a rotten profession, since all it took was one episode of bad judgment to ruin the entire season and possibly your career.

Bud Tice knew exactly what I had done but tried to make me feel better by saying it may not be as bad as it looks. But Eddie Abramowski, the head trainer, told me that it was a third-degree separation, which is the worst and most painful. Tony Greene came in from practice, and I asked him to drive me to the hospital. As Tony was getting dressed, Knox came in to see me. He said, "I just want to tell you not to worry. I'm not going to put you on injured reserve. Whatever the hell they do to you, I'll definitely keep you on the active list. We'll be one man short on the roster, but we'll be ready for you when you're healthy again." Had he put me on injured reserve I'd have missed the whole year.

Knox really made me feel good, and I said, "I promise you I'll be back soon. I heal fast and I'm not going to miss the whole year." We hadn't even started our preseason yet, so I had four weeks of preseason games as a head start in which to heal.

What was particularly uplifting was Knox adding, "Don't worry about your contract. We'll take care of that." That was a ray of hope before discovering how extensive the injury was.

When the doctor finally examined me at the hospital, he tried to strap down my shoulder where it had separated from my collarbone, but the separation couldn't be reduced manually. "We have to operate," intoned the doctor, not knowing that these were not my favorite words to hear. At that time, on the east coast, the medical philosophy was to put a five-inch screw right into the acromioclavicular (AC) joint to secure it to the collarbone. Conversely, on the west coast, surgeons favored going in and cutting off the end of the collarbone, which eliminates the AC joint and prevents the shoulder from ever separating again. The legacy of this operation is that your shoulder will always be weaker. What I didn't know at the time was that it was a rare occasion when the AC joint was ever repaired permanently.

After that discussion, everything seemed to occur in a blur. I would've preferred Dr. Godfrey to operate on me, but Knox had released him the year before. Godfrey wasn't a coach's kind of doctor because he cared more about the players' health than whether they could get back on the field as quickly as possible. The current team doctor, Dr. Weiss was also an excellent surgeon and wanted to tackle my shoulder immediately. Before I had time to think about it, the nurses were prepping my shoulder for surgery. I remember the doctor saying to me right before I was put to sleep that this should turn out just fine. These were becoming very familiar but uncomfortable words.

When I awoke the following morning, I could not conceive of having worse pain than what I was feeling. It was diabolical. I couldn't move or do anything, and if I accidentally coughed or cleared my throat, I would break out in a sweat from the pain. Injections for the pain made me sick, and so for the next few days, I would live on Empirin with codeine every four hours. I phoned Marilyn and said with tears in my eyes, "I can't imagine making it through this entire day." I had a metal screw that went five inches into the shoulder. The damnedest thing about it was that the end of it stuck out about a quarter of an inch. My skin was on top of this protrusion, but it looked like the screw was going to poke through the skin at any moment. I was told that when they get ready to take it out, they will make a small incision to let the screw become visible, and then they will just unscrew it. It looked like something out of a Frankenstein film.

Rather than sit around bitching and moaning in Buffalo, I decided to fly home for four weeks. After a few days in California, Marilyn conceded that I was a royal pain in the ass. I mean, all I could do was to just sit and wait for this awkward-looking shoulder to heal. On Sundays I was completely unbearable. I couldn't stand watching everybody bounding around the field as I sat there like an invalid nursing something else back to health again. Naturally, I was miserable. The nice part was having Marisa around me. I remember seeing her get ready to slip one day, and as I reached down for her, I actually fell to the floor on the pinned shoulder. I didn't move and asked Marilyn to look at the shoulder to see if the pin had popped out. Thankfully, it remained intact.

When the Bills were playing the Chargers, I went down to San Diego and told Knox, "As soon as I get unscrewed, it won't take me long to be a hundred percent again." Ironically, the team played poorly that day. Butler had a pulled muscle and wasn't doing that well, so my absence was even more magnified.

So far, they had only played two in-season games, and I flew back with the team to wait one final week in Buffalo before I got my screw loose. When the time came, it was so bizarre, just like out of a horror film. Dr. Weiss had me lay on a table in his office while he shot a little local anesthetic into the shoulder. Then he cut into the protruding flesh and started to unscrew this metal rod. It felt like it was coming out of my neck or spinal cord, and it was grotesque watching this piece of machinery coming out of my body. When Weiss offered to give me more local anesthetic, I lied and told him I didn't need any. I had had this reputation for having a very high threshold for pain. Everyone used to say that Bobby Chandler never complains. I guess I got kinda swept up in that lie.

Now that the mechanical part was over, I could fall back into my private routine of rehabilitation. I didn't attend all the team meetings, which Knox, I'm sure, wasn't too happy about. I couldn't blame him for being upset. What I was really saying to the team was that I'd suffered a lot and just wanted to do my own thing until I was ready to join them.

I really worked hard on getting back in shape. My rehabilitation consisted of a myriad of shoulder exercises preceded by trying to "walk up a wall" with my fingers. This was done to get a full range of motion back into my shoulder, which was the toughest part.

Bud Tice had become almost my personal trainer during this period, since he spent most of his time trying to get Humpty Chandler back together again.

I'd go out and catch as many balls as I could while knowing

that I couldn't raise my arm very fast without pain streaking through my shoulder and neck. The idea of my getting hit near the injury was so frightening that I just had to put it out of my mind.

In midseason, we played our eighth game in Detroit. Knox put me in as a third wide receiver. But I was scared. I mean really scared. And it was because I knew in my gut that I wasn't ready to play yet. Unfortunately for me, Knox had manipulated me by doing the favor of not putting me on injured reserve. So I really owed him this game.

On the first play, I was running from the slot position inside Frank Lewis. As I ran down about ten yards around him and across the field, Joe threw it low and in front of me. It was exactly the same way the ball was thrown when I originally separated my shoulder. Don't ask me why, but I went down for it, and just as I grabbed it, the defensive back pinned my arms down to my sides. With his arms around me, I tried twisting the other way, and he drove my shoulder into the artificial turf. It was *déjà vu* time, sports fans. As soon as I got up, I knew my shoulder had separated again. My entire right side was shaking violently, and I couldn't control it as I hobbled off the field holding my arm.

The trainers and the doctor came over to me on the bench and asked if they could look at my shoulder. As they started lifting up my jersey, I yelled, "Get away from me. Just leave me alone!" You see, I just didn't want anyone to tell me point-blank that my shoulder had separated again. That was something I couldn't handle right then. I was practically sure that it had, but I was still hoping that it hadn't. After telling Knox that I couldn't go back in to play, I just sat on the bench until half time not allowing anyone to get near me.

In the locker room at half time, I confided to Tony that my shoulder was ruined again. Officially, the doctor took an x-ray, which confirmed my worst thoughts. "It's separated," said Dr. Weiss, "but doesn't look as bad as last time." That's what I needed, lots of encouragement. We were going into our ninth game of the season, and I was washed up for the year!

7

Westward Ho! The Raiders'
Newest Bounty—
Starting Over

Searching for love in the murky glaze of a half-empty coffee cup.
Neon-lit diners exposing character you'd rather forget.
Anxious nights masked by idle chatter.
    Just trying to find comfort in the cold, tattered cushions of a booth
  called home.
Food from a grease-caked grill, washed down by coffee that won't stay
  hot.
Taste is unimportant;
    The motions are just part of the ritual.
It's an ever changing scene.
    Visitors to the night lack authenticity.
    They pass through the morning with disdain for regulars.
    They'll be back and back.
The stench of the smoke-filled room becomes your favorite shirt.
A little warm-up on the coffee, Rose, it's time for a new romance.

—BOB CHANDLER
1978—Your Host Restaurant—4:00 A.M.
Buffalo, New York

They called it a second-degree shoulder separation. I drove all the way to Rochester for a second opinion, but he concurred with Dr. Weiss. Both doctors felt that putting my shoulder in a brace to reduce the separation would be useless. The consensus was to just let it go. Medicine could not work a miracle. I might have to go through the rest of my life without being able to use my right arm properly. The thought of this scared me to death.

It got worse. The following week, Knox put me on injured reserve. I was naturally a bit upset, but I also knew that he had no choice, since he was playing with one man short. (With a player on injured reserve, the team can place another player on the roster.) Marilyn begged me to come home and just call it quits for the season. But I couldn't do that. I needed to get this thing right while in Buffalo. I knew I had to build up my shoulder and arm from scratch, and I guess it was more psychological than anything else. I decided I'd be up shit creek if I waited until the following season to try to rehabilitate myself.

From that moment on, what there was left of my relationship with Coach Knox totally disappeared. I was as useless as the proverbial tits on a bull. He probably would've preferred that I went home, so as not to have had a constant reminder of the superfluous Mr. Chandler. Bud Tice spent all of his time after practice working on my shoulder and arm, and slowly the pain began to subside. It didn't really matter, because I was finished for the season.

I continued with my early morning radio show. Even though I wasn't playing, the fans still enjoyed the show and my candid comments. When I'd go out in the evenings, folks would still run up to me and ask if there was any chance I could come back this year.

By the last month of the season, I actually went out on the field and began practicing. And the shoulder felt pretty good. One morning, I got into the training room at 10:00 A.M., knowing that the entire team would be in the meeting, which began at 9:30. I was having my usual cup of coffee with Bud when Knox came around the corner and said, "Hey, listen, I want you at the team meetings. You're still a big part of this."

I replied, "Why should I go to those meetings and just sit there?" I realized that nobody was going to force me into those meetings. Knox could fine me, and I still wouldn't go. It was the only way I could handle the situation. I figured that I couldn't have survived this many seasons or have gone through what I did and not at least pretend I was a bit of a rebel. When I was playing, I gave everything I had for the team. When I was injured, I wasn't a nice or fun person to be around.

The only person who could tolerate me at this time was Tony Greene. He, too, was in an uncomfortable position, since he wasn't playing either. Knox had phased Tony out completely from the lineup. Tony's backup, Jeff Nixon, was playing, and playing very well. Unlike me at times, Tony handled everything with so much class that one would never suspect he felt bad.

Another reason that I wanted to get out on the practice field was my contract renegotiation. Ever since my first shoulder separation, I hadn't heard one word about my contract. I kept quiet, realizing that I was operating now at a distinct disadvantage.

At these practice sessions, Knox would occasionally get on me for not wearing hip pads, or knee pads, or would tell me to put my jersey over my jacket. Dumb things, but embarrassing nevertheless. Since I wasn't fitting in as one of Knox's guys, I started writing the scenario in my head about Tony and I being the next players to be traded. As painful as it was to be rejected like that, I couldn't fault Knox, especially since one year later—without us— he turned the team around. Once in a while, Knox would joke with me, but I always felt that he never really cared for me that much.

Funny thing about this profession: you can pour your heart into your playing and sometimes you're a big star; but when you're hurt, you become a drone, and it's as if you're a nonperson. Everyone treats you differently. One day you're a big shot, and the next day you're not. But you can still be a big shot again. It's as if your wife loves you one year and hates you the next.

Then, for some reason, she starts loving you again. It could drive anyone crazy.

While Knox was blowing hot and cold, I got the impression that the team's PR director, Bud Thalmann, had it in for me. Maybe it was because that was the popular thing to do as far as Knox was concerned.

I was beginning to feel uncomfortable doing my radio show, since I wasn't contributing on the field. I began to look at myself as somewhat of an outsider. Just about every night, Tony and Lou Piccone and I would go out for dinner and go to a club, and often we'd be out till 4:00 A.M. Tony and I would be a bit hung over at practice, but it didn't seem to matter, since neither of us was playing.

I was becoming disillusioned about everything. I hated being injured and I hated being away from my family. I'd rationalize in my mind that I hurt and therefore deserved a paycheck. My shoulder healed fairly well, with only the end of my collarbone sticking up about an inch where it had separated from the joint. Above all, I was getting tired of being invisible.

After making a special appointment to see Knox, I came into his office and said, "I think it'd be best if I left here." And son of a bitch, if he didn't agree with me. I hoped he would have begged me to stay, but he said, "I agree. You've been here a long time, and the change might do you good." He also let me leave a week earlier to drive my car to the west coast, and on top of that, he got real generous and gave me a Buffalo Bills' golf shirt.

I walked out of Knox's office feeling very conflicted. Here I was, only one reception short (295) and one touchdown short (34) of setting two all-time Buffalo Bills records, and I was walking away from the team. But I'd been through too much with this one team. I had endured through the regimes of five head coaches—each one trying out a new system. It was hardest of all to give up those records because of the hard work I'd put into them. But new records are set all the time, and it wasn't worth it to me to spend another whole year in Buffalo just to make history for a few seasons. My daughter, Marisa, was growing out of her infant stage and was becoming a delightful human being. I wanted to be closer to home this time around.

Getting Buffalo out of my system was another story. I really loved that town, with its inhospitable climate. Maybe it was because my most formative years, from the age of twenty-one to thirty, were spent there. The city had become a big part of my life and it was hard as hell to leave. I became very nostalgic as I packed my car. I even stopped by most of the restaurants and bars that had become my homes away from home and said good-bye to both the staffs and the patrons. Finally, driving home across country by myself gave me a chance to muse about those nine years—many of which were truly the best years of my life.

In retrospect, one of my biggest regrets is that I didn't have the opportunity of starting out together with Chuck Knox. Chuck came into a situation that was in complete disarray, and I was a spoiled, crotchety veteran who was simply tired of changes. Knox was and is a brilliant coach and motivator. Although I think we both have respect for each other off the field, we were sadly never able to translate that into an on-the-job rapport.

In late January, I met with Chuck Knox at LA's Century Plaza Hotel. He was en route to the coaches' convention, where he had promised to "shop me around" a little. When he returned to LA a week later, we met again; and he opened the conversation by saying, "Sorry, Bob, nobody's really interested in you."

I replied, "Well, don't sugarcoat it. Just tell me like it is!"

Getting serious, Knox was in a difficult position. He was aware that I was a relatively big attraction in Buffalo, since the fans considered me one of their favorites. Football had become show biz, and stars were needed to sell tickets. Even though he wanted to get rid of me, Knox also didn't want to do something that would piss off the Buffalonians, by giving me away for nothing. At this meeting, he was more cooperative than I'd ever seen him. Asking me where I preferred to go (as if I had a choice), I said, "My first choice would be Oakland, then San Diego, San Francisco or Los Angeles."

Knox laughed aloud. "The one coach who showed the most

interest in you at the convention was Tom Flores!" Flores was coaching Oakland, and we knew each other from the very first year with Buffalo where he was the receiving coach for that season.

I was in seventh heaven when I left Knox. Later, when I thought more about it, I realized I was just being naive again. I was no Cinderella, and I could just as easily end up freezing my cojones in Green Bay or possibly Cleveland. It was very difficult for me to comprehend that nobody was interested in me. I knew it was because of my injuries, but this definitely contributed to my self-doubts. Knox, in his inimitable way, only reinforced these.

Knox phoned me the following week, saying, "I'm trying to work something out with the Raiders. All that they've offered is a sixth-round draft choice, which isn't much. Their biggest worry is your physical condition." Then came the hardest blow of all when he added, almost as an afterthought, "Why don't you go up there and let 'em look at you. Put yourself on trial."

It's not often that a guy who's caught more passes than any other guy in the NFL during the past four years has to go to try out. I knew that standing behind my pride would get me nowhere, so I acquiesced, hoping that Flores would remember me fondly.

When I arrived at the Oakland Raiders' offices, Tom Flores clarified things by saying, "Bob, I don't want you to think this is a tryout. All we want to know is if you're physically okay."

While I was in Oakland, I got to meet Lou Erber, the receiver coach. He really made me feel good when he said, "Would we ever love to have you on this team. We've always thought that you were the closest thing to Fred Belitnikoff!"

I was sent back to Los Angeles to be examined by Dr. Rosenfeld, who really worked me over. He told me that my shoulder was separated so severely that, from the x-rays, it almost looked like it had been resected. The irony was that after enduring months with that monster pin in my shoulder, the second separation had virtually eliminated the AC joint anyway. Rosenfeld seemed reasonably satisfied with the condition of my knees and back. The clincher was that the doctor had gone to USC and remembered me there. Afterward, Rosenfeld phoned Al Davis and told him: "Take a chance with Chandler. He's had his injuries, but he's going to help you so much that it will really pay off." Rosenfeld went out on a limb and did me a big favor.

It was hard for me to concentrate on my studies at law school that spring because of the various machinations going on about my football career. Whenever I started feeling good about going with the Raiders, I would get shot down emotionally with phone calls from Knox. He claimed he was doing his best to make a fair trade, but it was going too slowly for me. About a week later, Knox phoned to say that they were negotiating now to trade me for Phil Villipiano, a linebacker. Phil was one helluva linebacker for the Raiders who had played approximately the same number of years as I had. Phil had been injured the previous season and didn't play much, but in spite of that, he was extremely popular with the fans and players in Oakland.

The conversations between the Raiders and Bills went on and on, and I was getting edgy as hell. Finally, on what I considered a fateful day, Knox phoned and said, "It looks like the deal's going to be set tonight." It must've been set earlier because I got a message on the board at law school to call Tom Flores. I dumped my books, raced to the phone, and when he got on the line, Flores said rather casually, "What number do you want?"

For me, it was like catching the ring on the merry-go-round. After celebrating that night with Marilyn and my folks, I was determined to work my ass off until training camp. Al Davis had gambled on me, and I wanted to make sure that the Raiders were getting what they had hoped for.

With the Bills, I was going into the last year of a four-year contract which gave me $117,000 a year. Considering the fact that I didn't play an entire season, I wasn't in the best bargaining position to get a pay hike from the Raiders. It felt like I was starting my career all over again. Christ! It seemed that the past ten years had just gotten canceled out, and I was back in the position of proving to them again that I could play well.

The Raiders had a little training camp for receivers during a few days in May just to get the quarterbacks and receivers aligned with each other. So I ducked out of law school and went up to Oakland, California, to make my debut with other members of the team. I felt terrific and was probably in the best physical shape I'd been in a long time.

One of the first guys I met was Dave Casper, a tight end, who was All-Pro and, after only five years of playing, had become a legend in the league. Nicknamed The Ghost, partly after the cartoon character and partly because he was so elusive at getting open, he was one of the most fascinating guys I'd ever run across in the NFL. He was also outspoken. At an early practice, he walked over to me, and looking intensely into my eyes, he said, "Listen, when you run that in, come down and push the guy to his inside shoulder a little more. And don't forget to carry your hands in a little better position." I thanked him for the advice. Casper then walked over to Lou Erber and asked him who I was. Erber thought Casper was putting him on and finally identified me. Casper screamed, "No shit!" and came running back to me saying, "I'm really embarrassed, I'm sorry, and forget everything I said." I was laughing my ass off as he explained that he had no idea that I was who I was, particularly since I was running around showing off like a rookie.

While I was really eating up everything at this minicamp, I later learned that Chuck Knox had called my best friend, Tony Greene, and told him that after going through a player evaluation, they decided to terminate his contract with the Bills. Tony phoned me with the news when I got back to LA. Worse still, Tony learned that no other team in the NFL would offer him a tryout in camp. In a word, he was blackballed! I immediately asked the Raiders management and was told that they wouldn't consider him at this time. What the hell did Tony do to deserve this? I could only assume that someone had put the word out that Tony was into drugs, which he wasn't. He was still playing well, and he had been voted by the players as captain of the team.

Someone had given Tony a bum rap and the damned thing stuck. I remember Mike Shaw, the assistant public relations guy for the Bills, telling me last season that there was a meeting which brought up the possibility of certain players being involved with drugs and that Tony and I were mentioned in that group. What incredible bullshit!

The team doctors would shoot all of us up with Novocaine or feed you codeine just to enable us to play, and afterward we'd be given Butazolidin or Indocin as an anti-inflammatory precaution. That in itself was major drug abuse, and it was routine. The guys who got into recreational drugs kept it to themselves initially. By 1978 and 1979, cocaine had become more commonplace in professional sports as it had across the country with people who could afford it. I was never aware of any drug problem with the players, since it was a very private matter, although there were rumors about drugs constantly.

After hearing the bad news, Tony became desperate and went to a few teams for an unsolicited tryout. He would run a forty-yard dash for them in 4.5 seconds, and then the teams would just say, "We'll be in touch with you." He finally got a job with Mobil Oil which paid about $17,000—a pretty small yearly wage after getting $125,000 playing pro football. But Tony handled his comedown with the same class he handled everything else. I would speak to him nearly every day during the season, and he never complained about anything. It's an admirable trait, and Tony, who is the godfather to my daughter, Marisa, is someone I can never forget.

Everything about the Raiders was diametrically opposed to what I'd experienced with the Bills. Management wanted forty-five individuals to play well on Sunday. They didn't care if you dared to be different, if you wore thigh pads or hip pads to practice, or if you lined up perfectly to do calisthenics. Having read so much about Ted Hendricks, John Matuszak, Gene Upshaw, Art Shell, Cliff Branch and many others, I felt like a star-struck kid among them.

At the first team meeting every guy had to stand up and give his name, school and position. It is always a somber affair. In Buffalo we would always stand up as if at attention. Here, it was like being at a circus where every player said something goofy or just screwed up. Matuszak was dressed in solid black, wearing huge sunglasses, and appeared to be three sheets to the wind, while Hendricks had had a few too many himself and didn't mind letting everyone know about it. I ran out of the meeting and quickly phoned Marilyn, saying, "This is where I should have been playing for my entire career."

Every day held a new revelation for me. It wasn't just the football that excited me. It was everything! At practices the players would work their butts off. When you weren't working, you could sit down on the ground, usually on your helmet or even lying on some practice dummies. These breaches in football etiquette were new to me, because the Bills had been so strict in following arbitrary rules. More importantly, the passing game was the greatest, with beautiful conditions for receiving. I was never so damned happy with football as I was at that moment. The only sadness I felt was when I thought of Tony Greene. Of all people, he had deserved this kind of team.

This may sound trivial, but after wearing number 81 for nine years, I was a little hung up about choosing another number. (My number was being worn by Morris Bradshaw, another receiver, who had been there for several years.) I took number 85, which seemed like a real fat number to me. It felt as if I'd changed my name, since every time I'd give an autograph in Buffalo, I'd also sign my number.

During training camp, I roomed with Dan Pastorini at the El Rancho Tropicana Motel in "beautiful" downtown Santa Rosa. We had long practices during double days, but they were fun because everything was much looser and more relaxed. Of the five different receiver coaches I'd had, Lou Erber was the one man with whom I felt the most comfortable. Besides being a terrific coach, he was a real friend. In fact, every once in a while, Lou and I would go out and drink beer together after the curfew check. And what a fiasco that curfew was. A different coach would be assigned to check each night. Curfew was at 11:00 P.M., and the coaches would check our rooms at 11:15. At exactly 11:20, there was more vehicle noise outside the motel than at the Indianapolis speedway as we all drove off to our favorite bars. Local Santa Rosans would flock to the bars at 11:30, since they knew that's where they would find the Raiders.

During the first week of training camp, I was working so hard at practice that I didn't feel like staying up late. My roommate, Pastorini, was just the opposite. Dan was new that year, having been traded from Houston for Kenny Stabler. But Dan was in the category of Hollywood stars, since he had been dating Farrah Fawcett and was married at one time to June Wilkinson. As a friend, he would do anything for me, but when he wanted to raise hell, he could do it with the best of them. Anyway, he was anxious to go out after curfew, and I resisted a bit at first because this was all very new to me and I didn't want to wreck something I had waited so long for. But I didn't resist too hard. We snuck out of the motel at 11:30 and went to a little tavern called the Music Box. Inside, at the bar, were Lou Erber, my receiver coach, and Sam Boghosian, an offensive line coach. Since this was my first time out, I felt very awkward and a bit like a high school kid that just got caught cutting class. Lou broke the ice, saying, "It's about time you guys got your asses out of that motel room. It'll drive you crazy sitting there all the time. Have a beer and relax." So we sat there and drank with them until 1:30 A.M. For me, it was a scene out of *North Dallas Forty*.

Unfortunately, I couldn't carouse every night like Pastorini could. A couple of nights Pastorini never came back at all, so I would get on the phone and start calling places, asking where Dan was. Usually, he'd run out on the field, looking like shit, after we'd started practice. The son of a gun would practice and work hard, collapse in the late afternoon, and go out again the very next night.

Comparing the Raiders' regime with the Bills' was like comparing night and day. Oakland's management was one of the few in the NFL that treated players like men. No one was standing over you and forcing you into a particular mold. Instead, you were given the leeway to be whatever you wanted to be, and this was channeled into our performance. We were proud to be Raiders and wanted to do justice to the team that gave us so much freedom.

By our first preseason game, I was still working my way up the ladder. Going in during the second quarter, I made a couple of good catches and ran my patterns well. I knew that if I could manage to stay healthy during this year, I would soon be starting for Oakland. Morris Bradshaw, a starting receiver, realized that I was brought in to fill a void—not as a rookie or a guy who hadn't proven himself. I did start in the third preseason game, and I'll admit that I was really at the top of my game. It was like a fantasy fulfilled, since I'd followed the Raiders as a kid and always wished I could be one of those "big bad guys of the world."

In my last conversation with O.J., he told me about a condominium he owned in San Francisco, and damned if he didn't offer it to me for the entire season. It was on Russian Hill and was absolutely magnificent, with a panoramic view of the entire city. My thruway Exit 56 Motel days were gone forever.

By another coincidence of fate, the guy who'd been with the radio show that I had done back in Buffalo, Sandy Beach, moved to San Francisco to join one of the better FM stations, KYUU. He pushed for my doing another radio show. However, this time I couldn't just roll over in bed and discuss the Raiders in a semiconscious state. This time I had to get up early, go to the station, and broadcast live at 7:45 and 8:45 A.M. I then taped another program, which was run that same afternoon, and gave me quite a bit of exposure.

Before I started the program, I figured I should ask Al or someone in the organization for permission. I first asked John Herrera, one of the assistant PR people, who went to Al Davis and got a resounding "no." Now, Al Davis is truly one of the recognized geniuses of the NFL. Owning less than 50 percent of the team and having been with the Raiders for fourteen years, Davis has total control and makes the final decision on everything. This man lives a life devoted to the Raiders. Watching our films eight hours a day, he was one of the innovators of the passing game. Choosing silver and black uniforms, he perpetuated that "bad guy" image, and let it be known that he welcomed outcasts and castoffs from every other team in order for him to give them their last chance. Thus, every player felt that Al had gone out on a limb for him, and consequently the players played their best for him. He made sure that his team went first class everywhere, that nobody felt they were getting screwed on their contracts, and generally that all the variables which could cause the team not to concentrate were eliminated. All he wanted us to do was win football games.

The results of this philosophy created the closest team with which I'd ever been associated. I mean there were forty-five totally different guys covering a wide spectrum of backgrounds, interests, and ages. These guys would still get into fights at practice primarily because of the intense competition. But nobody held grudges after practice; instead, they would all just laugh about it. The team's mutual friendship knitted us into a formidable machine that would eventually go on to capture another world championship.

Getting back to my radio show, I finally got up the nerve to ask Al point-blank. He said that he didn't want to start a precedent that would interfere in any way with the players' concentration. I explained that from my experience in Buffalo, I could put it in perspective and not let it affect my playing. Reluctantly, Al agreed. That in itself was a big vote of confidence for me. It suddenly occurred to me that Al Davis considered me more as a dividend than a possible liability.

8

Catching Super Bowl
Fever—The Pinnacle

Sometimes when you're down
And you've sunk to your lowest mark
Brace yourself, wipe off that frown,
And set your jaws to attack like a shark.
Not confronting your failure will make you a clown,
With the spotlight on but always in the dark.
You must have better qualities pound for pound,
So face up and sing like a lark.
It may rain, but you'll never drown
For clear skies bring sunshine to the park.
Now you're up and no longer bound
By those awful chains that had you down.

—BOB CHANDLER
1979—Buffalo General Hospital
Buffalo, New York

When I started playing for the Raiders, I vowed that Marilyn and Marisa would come to visit often. It only took forty-five minutes by plane to get to the Bay Area from LA instead of those five-hour cross-country flights. Living in O.J.'s gorgeous condominium, I now had a special place for my family to visit, which was a far cry from the seedy motel where I spent many years in Buffalo. I was making an effort to have my family more involved with my football life, and I could see how much happier Marilyn was. But whenever Marilyn would come up for a long weekend, she would always leave before Sunday's game because it caused her too much anxiety to watch me on the field.

Her first trip up to the Bay Area during the preseason did nothing to silence these fears. It was the third preseason game versus the New England Patriots. Raymond Clayborne, the Patriots' left corner, and I never got along too well. It all started several years earlier in New England. After catching a pass downfield, I was walking back to the huddle with Clayborne yelling obscenities in my ear. This happens so often that it never really bothers me since I usually ignore it. This time, I made the mistake of looking at Clayborne, and as I stared at him, he spit in my face. Now, in my many years in the NFL, I had never had that happen to me. As far as I was concerned, it was disgusting and certainly above and beyond what is considered tolerable psych on the field. So I swung at Clayborne, hitting him in the side of the head. The official just saw me swing without having seen Raymond spit. Therefore, I got the fifteen-yard penalty for unsportsmanlike conduct.

Joe DeLamielleure saw how pissed I was and asked me what had happened. I told him, and he was furious. Ferguson called a pass play, but Joe grabbed him by the jersey, telling him to forget it and instead run the ball toward Clayborne. When Ferguson did this, Joe pulled and led the way. He tried to grab Clayborne and choke him to death. The officials pulled Joe off, and Raymond took himself out of the game for a while—to save his life.

Since that day, Raymond and I had had a running feud on the field. In this particular preseason meeting, a ball thrown by Plunkett was intercepted on the other side of the field from me. Out of the corner of my eye, I saw Clayborne coming at me. He went right for my knees. Trying to avoid him, I jumped and twisted my back. And there I lay on the field for what seemed an eternity since I found that I could not stand up at all! Back in the training room, Dr. Rosenfeld tried to manipulate my back, but nothing seemed to help the pain. When they told me I was being sent off to the hospital to be set in traction, I pleaded with the doctor to let me go back to the hotel with Marilyn since this was her first trip up and I hadn't seen her in six weeks. He replied that Al Davis didn't want to take any chances, so I had to go. He did add that they would happily supply an extra bed in my hospital room so that Marilyn could spend the night with me.

Marilyn was shellshocked. By this time, she just wanted to fly back to Southern California. But she reluctantly agreed and spent her first night in the Bay Area in the hospital. The next morning, I tried for nearly two hours to stand up before the doctor came in. I wanted to convince them that I was well enough to take Marilyn out for breakfast and then to the airport. The doctor told me I was crazy, but he let me go. It was difficult convincing Marilyn over breakfast that this was going to be OK and that she shouldn't worry as things were going to be different this year. What Marilyn never knew was that after I dropped her off at the airport, I checked back into the hospital for more traction on the old spine.

That year Marilyn developed a routine for watching the games. Her closest friend from Whittier, Marla, would come over to our house wearing her number 85 jersey. They would mix a couple of stiff drinks and then watch the game. If it looked like I was in jeopardy, Marilyn would go into another room without television. Whenever something good happened, Marla would yell and Marilyn would come in to watch that moment. The overall fact that I was playing well and had no new injuries tended to soothe Marilyn's nerves.

In spite of my infatuation with the Bay Area, I was still experiencing withdrawal pangs for Buffalo. I would call the trainer, Bud Tice, at least once a week, and he would fill me in on the latest skinny out there. I missed Tony and Lou Piccone and those wonderful evenings spent in town.

It was a poignant experience for me to return to Buffalo when the Raiders played the Bills early in the season. Some of my old teammates met me at the airport, and there were TV cameras, interviews, and all kinds of exciting stuff going on. At the game, I was introduced and received a standing ovation from my old fans. When I saw Chuck Knox, we were on the best of terms. A month earlier, when the Raiders had cut two good ballplayers, I told them to talk to Buffalo and phoned Knox to recommend these guys. Buffalo picked them up and they played extremely well for Knox. With Knox having done me such a big favor to match me up with Oakland, I figured I owed him one—or two!

As special as that 1980 season was with the Raiders, there were a couple of unhappy experiences also. My new friend, Dave Casper, was an incredible free spirit. He was definitely listening to a different drummer. He would come out to practice wearing his football shoes but with no socks on; and always during practice, whenever he had the ball in his hands, he would sometimes kick it over the fence for no reason at all. He had some enormous problems—it was rumored that he was being sued, among other things—and he seemed to be on a binge of self-destruction. He would arrive at some games wearing a three-piece suit and a hat, while at other games he'd show up in a Hawaiian shirt and Japanese thongs. As Dave and I got to be better friends, I realized that he played harder than anyone on the team and was also the most modest about his obvious talents.

Casper's self-destruction got worse. On some days, he'd never show up for practice, and he kept staying up night after night until he seemed to me to become somewhat disoriented at times. Davis traded Casper to Houston right in the middle of the season! This came as a surprise to almost everyone, although all of us knew how Dave was abusing his body to the point where he could barely function.

The team had a superb backup tight end, Raymond Chester, who took over full time and really became a team leader. Raymond was a first-round draft choice who had been playing as many years as I had. Over a dispute with the Raiders, Raymond had been traded to Baltimore, which he likened to serving a prison sentence. He played well enough to become All-Pro, and when his option was played out, Al brought him back to Oakland. This was unheard of in the NFL. Once a guy was traded, he usually never returned to his old team. But Davis wrote his own rules and believed that if one of his former players was still playing a fine game of football five years later, then, by God, he would just take him back.

Al Davis was unique in other ways. By this time, it was alleged that a good many of the players in the NFL were abusing alcohol or drugs. Ostensibly, the NFL encouraged men with these problems to seek help in hospitals or clinics. The Catch-22 was that after a man got help to kick these habits, his fear was that he would be washed up on the team and generally blackballed from the rest of the league. As far as Davis was concerned, any man who sought help would automatically be accepted back on the team.

As I've said before, guys could easily slip into drug habits because of the nature of the game. The pain-killing drugs administered before games didn't give you a high feeling; they just made numb those parts of you that felt lousy. However, it was that very act of using artificial means to give you peace of mind while you worked that caused so many men to break down those natural barriers and feelings about drugs. When you finished a game, you felt that you owed it to yourself because you survived. You wanted to celebrate because you had that natural high which requires rewarding yourself. After a while, the player rewards himself, not necessarily for a job well done, but just because he came through the game in one piece. Then it gets to the point where he also does drugs just to make him feel better when the team loses. Finally, there can be nothing to celebrate, but taking drugs is something one gets used to on a Sunday night after the game.

There was also an attitude that many players had that they could recover from whatever they did the night before. Athletes are very tuned into their physical being, but because of their youth and being in top physical shape, they're not terribly accurate in knowing if they're functioning properly. It can turn into a vicious circle, since the guys who aren't functioning because of the drugs get depressed by that fact, and then take more drugs to become happy.

Cocaine was popular and generally available because dealers knew that football players had money. It was all part of their fast life-style.

Interestingly, during the past year or two, the attitude toward cocaine has changed, as team members have watched other guys acquire problems. When freebasing came in, guys who were partaking were becoming absolutely paranoid. I mean, they would lock their doors and sometimes even put up barricades just to keep out anyone who might be watching them. NFL security guys started policing the drug situation, and usage went down. The security men claimed that they could always spot a cocaine user while watching films of a game, since a heavy user was not supposed to be able to tolerate contact. So when a tough physical player starts shying away, he's suspect.

Another drug deterrent was the lectures given by Carl Eller, one of the great players for the Minnesota Vikings. Eller lost everything he had, every dollar he made and his entire family, because of his drug problem. Now, he goes out and lectures various teams in the NFL. He also runs a hotline which players can use to get advice on where to get help. While many teams didn't allow Eller to speak to the players for one reason or another, Al Davis welcomed the visits and really put out the word for every Raider to listen to Eller.

Davis' style touched everything we did in Oakland. After every home game, Davis would host a party at the Hilton Hotel for the players and their guests whether we won or lost. There was always a great buffet dinner and as much wine and beer as one wanted. What had always bothered me in Buffalo was losing a game meant every player would kind of slink out of the stadium almost hiding his head in shame. It was as if we were forced to be sad. That year in Oakland we didn't lose very often, but when we did, the prevailing attitude was that we did the best we could and nothing more could have been asked of us. When the game was over, it truly was over!

One weekend my parents drove up to the Bay Area on their way to Canada. They came to a game where we took a beating. I was supposed to meet them in the Coliseum parking lot, and when I did, they were standing there not knowing where they had parked their car. I told them to wait there, and I got into my Mercedes and drove through the parking lot looking for their car. Not finding it, I drove slowly back to where my parents were, and out of the blue, some drunk comes flying through the parking spaces and runs smack into the side of my car. I was totally shellshocked and just sat in my car shouting obscenities to myself. When I finally emerged from the car, the drunken guy screams at me that I was speeding. As a policeman walked over, some other guy stepped forward and proceeded to tell the cop that "this punk kid in the Mercedes was going way too fast and rammed his car into the other man's." Then this guy gives the old drunk his card, which identified him as an attorney. I blew my top until the cop said he saw the incident also and told me not to worry. After the policeman took down the vital statistics, I looked over at my Mercedes and saw this incredibly fat lady sitting on the hood of my car. I said in exasperation, "Would you mind getting off my car?" She replied, "Asshole, I'm glad he hit you. The way you guys played today, you deserved it!"

After losing that game, we surged forward winning nine games in a row. We'd always come back in the fourth quarter, and our defense really started playing unbelievable football. Pastorini broke his leg in an early season game and seemed destined to spend the rest of the season on the bench. But the rest of us all stayed healthy. I mean, everyone always had his aches and pains from bruises, dislocated fingers and fractured ribs, yet they all kept playing until we actually finished tied with San Diego for the best record in the American Conference.

Because of the tie-breakers, the Chargers won our division. So we were the "wild card," which meant we had to win four games instead of three to go to the Superbowl. Getting into the playoffs was a big first for me, since I wasn't able to play in the playoffs when Buffalo got there. This season was particularly satisfying for me since I led the team with forty-nine catches. I had caught more passes in previous years, but never passes that meant as much. Ten of those catches brought us touchdowns, and many of them won our games. Funny thing, this was the first year that I didn't care about whether I'd make the Pro Bowl or not. I guess I grew up over the years and now could move ahead with a different set of priorities. I had reached my own private Nirvana with the Raiders, and winning awards or breaking records had become unimportant. In fact, I became less concerned with the number of passes I caught each game, just as long as we won. But it was important for me to show the public that when I left Buffalo, I wasn't through with football. I needed to show that to Buffalo and to Chuck Knox while, at the same time, I wanted to give Al Davis more than he ever bargained for.

Up to this point in the history of the NFL, no wild card team had ever won the Super Bowl. That's the kind of challenge that the Raiders liked. We played Houston in the first playoff game, and our defense was just superb. It was the first time I got to meet Kenny Stabler, as he was traded from Oakland the year I came aboard. He came into our dressing room an hour before the game and said to me: "I really wanted to meet you 'cause I've heard so many good things about you. Casper talks about you every day, saying that you're the best in the game. Goddamn, I would've loved to have played with you." This is the guy who threw to Belitnikoff for at least twelve years. Stabler received bad press, but on the field he was incredible. Most of the stories were probably true about how Stabler would show up for a game a bit hung-over; yet, after being fed coffee, he would step onto the field and play magnificent football. Anyway, I couldn't get over the fact that Stabler wanted to meet *me* especially, since he'd been my idol for so long that I nearly asked him for his autograph.

As the season wound down, Pastorini was becoming more and more paranoid about the coaches and front-office guys ignoring him. Dan believed that his leg had healed and he wanted to play. Besides his antipathy for Pastorini, Davis knew instinctively that Dan's coming back would cause problems for Jim Plunkett.

Plunkett was doing magnificently. He had taken our team to the playoffs; therefore, Davis didn't want to add any extra pressure on him by having Pastorini sitting in the wings waiting for Plunkett to fuck up.

I felt a real kinship with Dan because we came to the Raiders at the same time. He had a bad reputation as a hell-raiser which was generally tolerated by the Raiders, despite the fact that Tom Flores personally never appreciated that type of guy; yet, at the same time, Flores along with the rest of us really respected Dan's abilities as a quarterback.

Until the end of the season, which wasn't far off, Pastorini had to be content with being a nonperson. Having had plastic surgery due to an unfortunate automobile accident, his face now bore the scars of his recklessness. I felt so sorry for him as I watched him swallow his pride and cheer us on through the playoffs. This was the first time in his life that he wasn't a part of things, and the team's climb to glory only accentuated his feeling of having failed.

In spite of Dan's off-field activities, there has never been a tougher, smarter competitor. During his nine years in Houston, he took beatings that no quarterback could have endured, and he kept coming back. He was a young, talented kid who grew progressively tougher and more calloused after each beating he suffered during those years. Dan was my closest friend on the team, and even though he had so many problems during this time, he was one of the most generous and caring friends anyone could ask for. As a player, one never doubted Pastorini's ability and leadership when he lined up behind the center.

After beating Houston, we flew back east to play Cleveland. Since we were playing past the end of our regular season, Davis couldn't get the usual chartered plane that we considered our flying home-away-from-home. United Airlines offered Al a 727 to fly us to Ohio, but Al Davis said he didn't want to downgrade his team in such a cramped aircraft. In his typical style of doing things first class, Al chartered us a giant 747. Each man had his own section of seats on the plane, and other amenities included first-run movies and eighteen stewardesses falling all over us. The only thing that wasn't allowed was alcohol. Violating that rule meant a stiff $1,000 fine. Davis later rationalized this expensive decision by saying that he knew the weather was bad in the Cleveland area, and he wanted his men not to be unduly upset by a bumpier ride in a smaller airplane. As it turned out, Cleveland *was* in the midst of a roaring blizzard, but we landed so smoothly that I didn't even know we had reached the ground—and *I* am definitely not crazy about flying in snowstorms..

Now, Cleveland in the best of weather conditions has one of the worst playing fields in the country. It happens to be a grass field, and I know I've always extolled grass over the man-made stuff. But only when the weather's relatively decent. When it freezes over, it can be horrendous. By this time, late December, any vestige of grass had long gone, which left a dirt field frozen harder than a rock. Taking into consideration the wind-chill factor, it was approximately fifty degrees below zero on the day of our game. Those winds whip across Lake Erie and bring a chilling blast to Cleveland and vicinity. To those of us used to the temperate climate of the Bay Area, it was murder. I wore long underwear, taped up every perforation in my helmet, put a layer of Vaseline on my hands before donning rubber surgical gloves, over which I wore leather golf gloves.

The game was a close one. We were ahead by two when Cleveland started a push down the field late in the fourth quarter. On the fifteen-yard line, we were sure they were going to go for a field goal. Instead, their quarterback, Brian Sipe, dropped back on third down to throw the ball. He was trying to go to Ozzie Newsome—their great tight end—in the corner of the end zone. At the last second, Mike Davis, our safety, intercepted the pass, giving us control of the ball and a victory. Afterward, I had to sit in the shower for forty-five minutes just to revive both my little fingers and all my toes, which had gotten frostbite.

Thank God, the AFC Championship Game was being played on the west coast. We went down to San Diego to play the Chargers, and the whole city of San Diego went bananas. There were huge parades, and the day before the game was consecrated in holy tones as "Charger Day." The city was acting as if their team had already won the championship. Super Bowl Fever had overtaken the place. All of this hoop-de-dah really fired us up. Our tight end, Raymond Chester, ran around getting everybody fired up before the game. Incredibly, Raymond had never done this before, and we were all touched by seeing how much winning this game and putting our total effort meant to him.

During the past season, we had played the Chargers twice, with each team winning one game. Now, we were so fired up that we thought we were invincible. It turned out that our defense played very tough, and we ultimately beat them 35 to 28. I'll never forget watching the clock tick off the last five seconds of the game. I felt twelve feet tall thinking that everything that my teammates and I had done was now finally going to pay off. It was as if my entire decade of pro football had reached a culmination at that magical moment. Whether we went on to win the Super Bowl or not, it almost didn't matter, since this moment of unbridled happiness would never come again in my lifetime.

The Super Bowl was almost anticlimactic after beating the Chargers. As usual, Mr. Davis did his thing with incredible style. He wanted all of us to bring our families to New Orleans because he knew how much it meant to each of us. And he picked up the tabs. I had my parents, my sisters, and Marilyn come out, and it was a once-in-a-lifetime experience for all of us.

There was an enormous difference between us and our opponents, the Philadelphia Eagles. Their coach, Dick Vermeil, went completely overboard during those weeks before the game because he wanted to win so badly. He had his team working harder than ever before in the season. They had to endure two practices a day, which can really knock the shit out of you, and he kept the drills so constant that, by the time of the game, I believe his team was weary of the game and just wanted the season to end mercifully. On the other hand, Tom Flores saw that we practiced only once a day, which gave us time to relax and to enjoy the city of New Orleans. He was strict about our keeping regular hours—New Orleans can be such a distracting city, beckoning all of us to play through the night, and we needed to stay in top gear.

The Super Bowl was like the Academy Awards with its comparative quotient of glamour. Sixty million fans were watching us on their TV screens, and to most of the guys out there on the field, it felt like the Kentucky Derby, the Indy Five Hundred, and the heavyweight title bout all rolled into one. I was concentrating so hard on doing what I should be doing that the game sped by almost too fast.

After winning the Super Bowl, 27 to 10, we were down in our locker room, and the press charged in, buttonholing about ten or twelve players for comments about the game. We had to go over to a press room which looked like a banquet hall with all these little pedestals propped up. Each of us stood on a pedestal while the press threw questions at us. I remember one newspaper guy asking me, "All right, Chandler, this past season you've been a part of the easygoing Raiders with that hang-loose philosophy. How does it feel?" I answered by saying how much I had thrived in just that kind of environment. I felt I had paid my dues in the regimented atmosphere at Buffalo over the years. I went on to say that this was the last stop for me and added, "Once you've played for the Raiders, you've gotten a taste of being treated like a man, with people allowing you to make your own decisions. Here, the importance is focused on performance on the playing field, which makes it damned difficult to play elsewhere." I guess I got carried away pontificating. After the press conference, I thought that the Raider philosophy was not the kind of program I would want my son to go through if he were in high school. At that age, regimentation is really necessary. But once a guy is over twenty-one, his value system is established, and he can be so incredibly nourished by being regarded as an adult.

9

Spleenless But Not Spineless—Downward and Outward

Coming of age brings rewards,
*   or so it seems.*
To be shackled with no thought
*   of trampled feet.*
What must one do to achieve a peace?
A game of no real concern steals these rewards,
*   Erasing sacrifices paid in full.*
Responsibility eludes us all, when decisions
*   are not ours to make.*
To be treated as a child
*   No regard for wrinkled brow*
*   Brings those results, and nothing more.*
Plug me in and I'll perform, until the
*   decision becomes mine to make.*

—BOB CHANDLER
1981—St. Luke's Hospital
Denver, Colorado

Most of us found our nerves were slightly frazzled from the tension of the Super Bowl. We took a couple of days just to rest up from the game and then we flew back to Oakland, where the city had a parade in our honor. Heavy rains didn't deter the thousands of people who turned out to welcome back the conquering Raiders. Nearly every player showed up, and each of us rode separately in a vintage classic car to a platform set up downtown where we were interviewed individually. Al Davis didn't show up for the festivities; as usual, he didn't want to steal the thunder from our moment.

Al Davis' gift to the players was a special Super Bowl ring that each of us was fitted for a few weeks earlier. Had we not won, we would've had AFC Championship rings instead. Each ring had approximately thirty-two diamond chips around two large diamonds in the middle in a silver and black (our team's colors) setting. What an impressive gift, with our names, positions, AFC Championship Game score, and Super Bowl score all engraved into it. We never knew what the rings cost Al, but we did find out later that they were appraised for insurance purposes at about $20,000 each.

The night of our Super Bowl victory party, as if that wasn't enough, I found out I had been picked by my teammates to participate in ABC's Super Teams in Hawaii. For years I would watch the Super Bowl teams competing and having the time of their lives in those events. For this particular year, the Eagles and the Raiders chose ten men from each team to represent them in the Super Teams games. I was very honored to have been selected along with John Matuszak, Ted Hendricks, Mike Davis, Raymond Chester, Kenny King, Ray Guy, Rod Martin, Jim Plunkett, and Lester Hayes. We were to compete in seven events, and I was scheduled to do all of them except the tug-of-war.

We flew over first class. It was interesting getting to know some of the Eagles who were on the same plane. They seemed to be very happy that the game was over, since their coach, Dick Vermeil, had decided to make their two-week preparation before the game similar to training camp. That meant practicing twice a day and enforcing a curfew every night. The players felt that if that was the way they were rewarded for winning the NFC Championship, they jokingly said they'd rather watch it on TV next year.

The first event was swimming, and I must say that if there is anything I can do better than anybody else in the NFL, it's swimming. It turned out to be a relay, and I swam one of the longest portions of 50 yards. We beat the Eagles mercilessly by a whole length of the pool. I never even needed to show them my blazing speed.

The next event was the track relay. I was the first leg, and I was damned nervous because wide receivers are supposed to be able to run pretty well. Luckily, I held my own against Randy Logan, an Eagle defensive back. The ace up our sleeve was having Mike Davis run the last quarter of a mile. Davis is a killer on the football field, and if there was anyone I would pick to run the 440, it'd be Mike. We were then 2 and 0 over the Eagles. The rules stated that you had to win four events, and then the winning football team would compete against the winning baseball team from the two teams that had played in the World Series.

We then went to the obstacle course, where five men would compete, and the total times would be added up. I got over the eleven-foot wall in good shape, but when I got to the monkey bars, my hands got stuck. (We Raiders were notorious for the stick'um that we wore on our hands during the season; it works great catching a football, but it sucks in an obstacle course.) I had to regroup but then I stumbled and tripped through the tires. Now, you have to remember that wide receivers go through tires on a regular basis during practice and are supposed to be very proficient at it. But since I fell behind on the monkey bars, I was trying a bit too hard in order to catch up. After that, there was a water jump, a high-jump bar, two hurdles, then the finish line. I ran it in 28 seconds with all of those mistakes, which wasn't too bad. As it turned out, we again beat the Eagles, by 0.5 second. The day was over, we were 3–0, and we felt we had it in the bag.

That night, Marilyn joined me and Jim Plunkett and his girl friend for dinner. Over the meal, Jim and I were counting the $15,000 as if we'd already won and as if we were going to compete against the winning baseball team. The baseball teams, incidentally, were the Kansas City Royals against the Philadelphia Phillies. (The kicker was having a team from Philadelphia on each roster.)

The following day, the Eagles beat us in volleyball and squeaked by us in a photo finish in the kayak race, which we felt we won. But we didn't make a big deal over it. After all, these games were being played for money and just for the sheer enjoyment of it all. The overall score was then 3–2, which really fired Philadelphia up. Their captain, linebacker Bill Bergey, and the rest of his team were definitely taking these games seriously. We sort of sat back looking at these guys and wondered what the big deal was. This was just supposed to be fun and games. I mean, *we* won the damn Super Bowl, that was the real game.

The next event was the outrigger canoe race in which we had to maneuver this crazy boat twice around a buoy. These two Hawaiian guys gave us pointers on how to handle the boat, but you had to have been there to believe how seven of our biggest guys and me all fit into that canoe without sinking. The Eagles killed us in that race, which evened up the score 3 to 3. Now we were beginning to worry a little bit.

The last event was the tug-of-war. Being exhausted from the outrigger race, Matuszak and Hendricks convinced the rest of us to have a few beers to build up our strength. No one seemed to question that logic. So we had a leisurely lunch and a few beers while the Eagles stuck close to their training regime in anticipation of the big event. Then they started chanting, which was a phenomenon we couldn't understand. They were so serious about beating us, and having so little fun trying to do it, that we were beginning to think these guys were real jerks.

I wasn't included in the eight-man team because they needed the most weight possible, and even with our biggest heavyweights, our team was still about 150 pounds lighter than the Eagles' team. We thought we were at a disadvantage, but we also figured that we beat 'em once before when it really counted so we could do it again.

The beach was jam-packed with the curious by the time we were supposed to start. Bob Cousey, of Boston Celtics fame, was the commissioner in charge of these events, and he was the man who handled all disputes. The object was to pull this enormous rope farther than the opposing team in an allotted time period. There was a flag in the middle of the rope, and there was a water hazard between the two teams. When the flag crossed either outside edge of the water hazard, just before that team was ready to go into the water, the event was over. Usually with two evenly matched teams, an advantage of a few inches during the time period will win it for you.

Watching the match, I could see that the Raiders' team was tearing its guts out. Just as the time was running out, our team gave a giant yank and pulled the flag over the halfway mark by a couple of inches. There was a whistle, and then five seconds later there was another whistle. While our guys were wrapping their bleeding arms in towels, Bergey, the Eagles' captain, was yelling and screaming in Cousey's face. He claimed that when the first whistle went off—which they believed was in error—they let up. Each captain went into Cousey's trailer with some ABC officials to view the film of the event. Afterward, Cousey ruled that it was a draw, and it must be done again in a half hour. Now our captain, Hendricks, as different as he may be, is truly one of the most honorable and respected men in the game, and he said to us that it was obvious that we had won on the first whistle and on the second whistle also. However, Bergey put up such a stink that Cousey was forced to do it over to eliminate any further arguments. All of our guys said screw it. We'd won, and we weren't about to go through the event again. We went into the hotel bar and started celebrating our self-proclaimed victory. At this point, Reggie Jackson, who was acting as a commentator for ABC, came up to us and gave a five-minute emotional speech about the importance of our going back out there and doing it again. He claimed that it would be considered a forfeiture. In the meantime, Philadelphia was out on the sand waiting patiently. Those guys had nothing to lose and everything to gain from a second tug-of-war. We got together and hashed it over again and again. We'd be determined to forfeit the event at one point, and then someone would argue that we shouldn't just give it to them. About an hour later, we went out to the beach to get the damn event over with. By that time, the Philadelphia team had left the beach in a huff, led by Bill Bergey, of course.

It was then that the uproar really began. We started yelling that we came back in good faith, and now we felt that Philadelphia had forfeited. Finally, we took the "law" into our own hands, and we stormed the trailer to view the film. We couldn't believe what we saw; it was evident that we had won. Hendricks went up to Cousey and very emotionally called him a gutless motherfucker; he also said that if the Raiders were ever to win another Super Bowl, they would never participate again in the Super Teams as long as Cousey was commissioner. Cousey knew he was in deep shit and finally said that the only way to settle this dispute was by doing the event over the following day.

The next morning we were supposed to be on the beach by 9:30 A.M., but we couldn't find Matuszak and Lester Hayes, so we didn't make it until 10:00. To the moans and groans of the Philadelphia contingent, we walked out in a straight single line like Rommel's troops. Suddenly, Bergey started screaming that our being late had caused us to forfeit. We told them that we were only 30 minutes late, for God's sake, and that we were sorry. We also said that this was supposed to be fun and games, so let's just do it. Bergey yelled, "It's over. You guys just lost." The real topper came when Cousey upheld the forfeit. So the whole fucking thing was over and we never got to even have a rematch of an event we had already won.

Later that day, one of the producers for ABC told me that Bob Uecker, one of their announcers, had to go back to the mainland. One of the ABC crew knew that I had a radio show in San Francisco and they asked me to help them out for the next round of games when Philadelphia went against the victorious baseball team. I was so pissed off by the way things were handled that I politely turned them down. I also thought I would look like a hypocrite interviewing Bill Bergey and laughing it up, slapping him on the back. I guess my blind loyalty to my teammates made me a little shortsighted regarding a future in broadcasting. After that, I never again heard from anyone at ABC. I was so proud of

ity again. A few days later, my dad and I flew back to Los Angeles, and my poor mother looked horrified as I stepped off the plane. I had lost ten pounds, couldn't stand up straight, couldn't walk fast, and since all my blood levels were still low, I was as pale as a ghost. I could read in my mother's eyes the message that I'd been damaged beyond repair, and she was hoping and praying that I would never play football again.

Marilyn and Marisa didn't blanch when they saw me looking like death warmed over. I think they expected me to look even worse. My goal at that time was to gain some weight and build up my blood levels by taking iron pills. Dr. Kirshenbaum and I were on the phone regularly, and he projected a timetable for when I could start working out again. I was still pretty weak when I watched the team play Minnesota in the Monday night game on TV. Morris Bradshaw played in my spot, and later they put in Malcolm Barnwell, who caught a 56-yard ball for a touchdown. After the announcer said some nice things about Barnwell, Frank Gifford and Howard Cosell both wished me a speedy recovery on the air. I knew at that moment that I had to get back on the roster as quickly as possible.

The one thing I was grateful for was having already done the *Playgirl* spread. My giant new scar, which ran all the way up my middle, was not very photogenic. My God, I thought, the issue with me was due out on the stands November 5. I sure as hell didn't want to still be on injured reserve when the magazine came out. The last thing I wanted was to be in the same trap that caught Pastorini, which was being a nonproductive player sitting around on injured reserve and then letting it all hang out in a nationally known magazine.

Two weeks later, I flew up to Oakland, and I confess that it might have been a little premature. But I was miserable at home and figured that Marilyn would have more peace of mind with me out of town. I had that urgent need to be around the team even though I didn't really feel a part of things.

I wasn't able to get O.J.'s apartment as he had already sublet it, so I found a studio apartment which rented for a thousand a month. It was stark with very little furniture and weird colors on the walls. Since there wasn't even a TV set, I went out and rented a small TV which had to be carried up for me, due to my delicate condition. That night I really became morose while watching TV and staring at the crimson scar on my midsection. I had to make a comeback and fast!

Why did I try to come back so many times? Why did I love this game so much? I never questioned the sanity of my comebacks. I only knew they were absolutely necessary to my survival. Football and being a player had become my personality. It had moved into me and given me strength, an inner strength that enabled me to deal with my own insecurities. Because of the punishment I had endured and the comebacks I had mounted, there was no question regarding my masculinity. To be able to do something that strips away those doubts and puts you above question physically had become my way of dealing with the world. That's why I had to come back.

According to Dr. Kirshenbaum's schedule, I started lifting weights at first and began gently riding a bicycle. The first time I started jogging (which was about three and a half weeks after my surgery), I swear I could feel things moving up and down inside of me.

For the first time I was real scared. I knew I had to come back and I knew everybody thought I was tough enough to get back on the field, but I wasn't sure. I had a tough enough time accepting that I would ever be the same after losing a vital organ. Even if I did heal up, how would I ever take another solid shot in the stomach? After Dr. Kirshenbaum had told me all my organs had contusions on them like a fighter's, and after they had pulled my intestines out and placed them back in, how could I go across the middle again with my usual reckless abandon to catch that crucial twelve-yard first down? These were some of the thoughts racing through my head as I jogged that first afternoon. I was told the sensations of things moving inside of me were normal, but the fears were real. Now I had to figure out a way to suppress them deep into my being, never to emerge—until late some night when I was alone and once again afraid.

Coincidentally, Dr. Kirshenbaum flew to San Francisco for a medical convention, and when we met, I asked him if I could start playing a little earlier than we had planned. But he reiterated that he wanted me to wait a total of seven weeks before playing or even before practicing.

Jumping the gun a little, I began practicing at the beginning of the sixth week. It was hard as hell for me to reach up for a pass, since I could feel sharp stretching pains in the sutured area. Wearing a flak jacket doesn't actually give you that much protection, but mentally you feel much safer knowing there's something protecting your midsection. That weekend I told Al Davis that I could hold the ball for field goals and extra points. Speaking to Kirshenbaum right before the game, I was told that it was a bit risky, and if I got hit in the stomach again, my incision could herniate and require more surgery.

Up until this game, the Raiders hadn't scored a point in the previous three games, which was an NFL record of sorts. I went in to hold for a 51-yard field goal attempt by Chris Bahr, which resulted in our first points in twelve quarters and the margin for an eventual win against Seattle. In the following week's game, I actually ran a few patterns in the game. In the third quarter, I ran a sideline pattern, planted my toes in bounds, stretched for the ball, and landed flat on my stomach. Getting up slowly, I felt wet in my stomach area and looked down to discover that the front of my jersey was becoming bloody. I had scraped a couple inches of scar tissue off the incision, and while it bled a lot, it hadn't opened up, thank God. For the next few weeks, the scar would scab over during the week and then would bleed in the game.

By the time we went to Miami to play the Dolphins, I was beginning to feel fairly good. Mind you, I wasn't in great shape, but I was getting some of my speed and quickness back. Don Shula saw me before the game and said, "When I saw them carry you off the field in Denver, I just said to myself that Chandler will be back in time to play Miami."

As November 5 rolled around, I was glad to be back on the field and showing the world my healing powers. I never told any of my teammates about the *Playgirl* spread. Naturally, I was a little surprised when I walked into the locker room and saw an entire wall plastered with my photos. Underneath the pictures was a large sign saying, "Our wide receiver, The Slut."

It was positively amazing how much noteriety fell upon me due to the magazine. All the Bay Area TV stations wanted interviews, and I appeared on the *A.M. San Francisco* program as well as a local late night talk show. A lady reporter came to my apartment to interview me for the nightly news. The response was mostly positive. Sure, I got a share of crank letters saying such things as, "We thought you were a Christian athlete, so how could you do this to yourself?" Other onion letters asked me how I could do this to my fans, my family, and the youth of America.

All of the guys would hang around me when I went to collect my Raiders' mail. You see, I was getting dozens and dozens of letters from girls who'd always enclose their snapshots—some of them were posed in the nude! It was incredible. The most memorable letter was written in a beautiful handwriting and lamented that I didn't show more. This person inquired if I had any other photos of athletes in the nude for a scrapbook. This individual also wondered if football players patting each other on the ass meant something more than congratulations. After requesting more nude photos of me, or any other players on the team, the person gave me his new address, which turned out to be marine boot camp. It was signed by a guy about to start basic training. Holy shit, that guy's platoon was going to be in for a rude awakening!

After the initial excitement died down, I started feeling a bit ambivalent about the magazine spread. On the one hand, I was delighted that people all over the Bay Area were recognizing me; and yet, I also felt a little embarrassed, like I should cover up. I felt very vulnerable all of a sudden, since people knew more about me than I wanted them to know, which was a strange turn of events. However, there never was a point where I wished I hadn't done it. Al Davis never really mentioned it, probably because I was once again producing on the field. He knew I was working hard to get back in top form and not lying around languishing in the publicity. The coaches all shook their heads, saying, "We knew you were weird, but this is too much!"

By the time we played Seattle again, I was almost in top shape, with four games left in the season. I scored a touchdown and caught a few passes. In the fourth quarter, one of our fullbacks was carrying the ball and broke through the middle. I was running down to get into position to block for him when he got hit from behind and the ball popped straight up in the air. I caught it on the fly and started to run when someone grabbed me from the side and landed on my left foot, bending it almost in half. I heard something snap and was sure that I'd broken my foot. Hobbling back to the bench, I cheered the team on to the touchdown, and then limped back onto the field to hold the ball for the extra point.

By the time the game ended, I couldn't put any weight on my foot at all. X-rays showed it to be a terrible sprain and no fractures, and although the doctor wanted to put my foot in a cast, I resisted because I had already missed too much of the season. Big hero! I could barely get my shoe on and definitely needed a cane. I tried damn near everything to relieve the pain—even the remedy of wrapping my foot in cotton, saturating it with DMSO, which is used on horses, putting a plastic bag on it tightly to capture the fumes, and hoping that this remedy wouldn't burn the skin off my foot.

For those last three games I would get shots of Xylocaine in my foot on Sunday to numb the pain, and when I ran, it felt like my foot was flapping beneath me. The anesthetic would begin to wear off by the fourth quarter, with my foot feeling like knives were stuck in it. Those last games were bloody murder. I'd phone Dr. Fink on Sunday nights to come over in the wee hours and give me Empirin with codeine because the pain was so great that I couldn't even put a sheet over my foot.

Mercifully, we got to our last game, which was on a Monday night against the Chargers and played in San Diego. I caught seven passes that game for a total of 128 yards, which was a personal high for the year. Toward the end of the fourth quarter, I was coming in for a hook, and Plunkett threw it when he shouldn't have. As both linebackers were converging in on me, I tried like hell to catch the ball until one of the linebackers, Cliff Thrift, smashed into my midsection, a bull's-eye right on my incision, and I was down and not breathing. I'm thinking to myself, oh God, why didn't I wear that flak jacket for protection.

Dr. Fink ran out to me as I lay there, thinking that my parents and wife were watching the TV camera zoom in on me, prone in a lifeless state. Fink had a wide grin as he stood over me and said, "Jesus, you look bad. How's your spleen? Is it feeling okay?" It struck me so funny that I started laughing, my stomach relaxed, and I started breathing again. Somehow, I managed to hobble off the field and realized that nothing inside me was ripped apart that time.

We lost that last game. Actually, the Raiders had a lousy year, with seven wins and nine losses, but that didn't keep us from celebrating over a few beers at Matuszak's house that night. I had packed up all my gear in my car and spent that night at the Hyatt House in Oakland prior to driving to LA in the morning. At around 3:00 A.M., I was feeling thirsty, so I went into the bathroom for some water. Turning on the light, I nearly died seeing a lump the size of a grapefruit coming out of my neck. I didn't know if I had a tumor or was hemorrhaging internally or something. I decided not to call Dr. Fink in the middle of the night, so I was awake the rest of the night and scared shitless. The next morning, I rushed to Fink's office where he diagnosed the problem as my rupturing a small vein which caused all the swelling. I walked out of the office with an ice bag strapped around my neck while hobbling with my cane.

Driving down on the interstate, I looked like some car had just run over me. As I drove, I reflected on the past season. Never before in my professional career had I gotten this beaten up. I mean, I had been through some tough seasons, but this one was the limit. I was beginning to question whether I was getting too old for the sport. Maybe things weren't healing quite as fast as before. Maybe I was getting brittle. At this point, the physical sacrifice for football seemed way out of proportion to the positive aspects of the game.

Until I got to spend a few days at home, I had never realized how deeply affected my daughter, Marisa, was by my injuries. You can't predict how a kid will react to anything, nor can you comprehend what's going on in the head of a four-year-old. She said to me shortly after I'd come back, "You know, Daddy, we're really gonna get that Perry Smith [the defensive back who hit me, rupturing my spleen]. We're really gonna sock him." Amazed because I'd never mentioned his name to her before, I told her that it wasn't really his fault. She replied, "Still, he hurt you pretty bad." Later, Marilyn played me a tape Marisa made while I was recovering in the Denver hospital. She sang some songs, made up a prayer, and ended it by saying, "I dream of a place where Daddy would always be there and where he'll never break apart." I thought, what have I done to this poor kid? All of her experience of me was that I was away most of the time and was getting torn apart.

After resting my foot for two weeks and getting no relief, I went to a well-known orthopedist in Whittier. Dr. Wagner took a few x-rays, and after careful examinations of both feet, he found a torn ligament and a hairline fracture in the left foot, which he promptly put in a cast up to my knee. The other foot, which had also required Xylocaine to keep from hurting, was to be operated on as quickly as possible for the removal of a Morton's neuroma: a thickening of the nerve caused by constant irritation. Before I had a chance to change my mind, I was in Whittier Presbyterian Hospital being wheeled into the operating room. Dear Jesus, I was getting so fed up with all of these surgeries.

For this surgery I got a local anesthetic, and from time to time I looked down at my foot, which was cut wide open. It was fascinating because it didn't seem like he was operating on me. He removed the Morton's neuroma and showed me that it was as big as a half dollar. After he closed me up, I was able to leave the hospital with one foot in a cast and the other in a bandage, and after hobbling around on crutches for a few days, I felt like I was more suited for a wheelchair.

The sutured foot healed quickly, while it took five weeks for the cast to come off the other foot. Very gingerly, I began to work out, using my feet, and slowly the soreness and stiffness subsided. It didn't even hurt anymore when I wore football shoes, and hopefully there would be no more Xylocaine, please God!

Having finished law school during the last off-season, I decided to take an acting class. No, I didn't think I could replace Robert Redford after getting a few letters extolling my bare ass in *Playgirl*. I was just being realistic about the options I had left after retiring from the NFL. I wasn't that motivated toward the legal profession, which precluded my studying for the bar exam. I had begun my legal studies feeling it was important to have a direction and a viable, credible alternative after football. As time progressed, I was very proud of my law school accomplishments but was becoming less interested in making it a career. It seems I had been bitten by the center stage, and I was developing a burning need to stay under the bright lights.

I had some exposure in broadcasting from my radio shows, and since my face hadn't been ground into hamburger so far, I thought about the possibility of getting into television sportscasting. This is a very competitive field, especially since three out of every four ballplayers truly believe they'll become the next Frank Gifford.

I was serious about the acting classes, since I needed to work on becoming more open and less low key in public. One good thing about this Hollywood acting school was that nobody in my class followed football closely, and therefore I could remain anonymous. Being unknown permitted me not to be stereotyped as the jock turned actor, and it allowed my instructors and classmates to view me without any preconceived expectations.

Playgirl magazine wanted me to go on a promotional tour to Philadelphia, Chicago, and my beloved Buffalo, where the magazine is printed. It was great to get back to Buffalo and look up some of my old friends, like Lou Piccone, John Leypoldt (a former kicker), Jim Braxton and Bud Tice. Even Tony Greene flew in from Boston for the weekend. In all of the cities, I was interviewed on the local version of the *Tonight Show* or the local morning show. The conversation always centered on my spleen, or lack of it, and the *Playgirl* spread. To liven things up, in Philadelphia they had me on a show with two Penthouse Playmates to talk about our mutual experiences in the buff.

It was like I became famous overnight. Charles Kurault did a CBS Sunday morning special on the spleen thing and *Playgirl*. I was presented as a sort of Renaissance man. Next, *Pro* magazine wanted to do a feature article on me and possibly a cover shot. Having already been contacted by Al LoCasale, who was Al Davis' right-hand man, *Sports Illustrated* was pushing to feature me in their July issue. They also wanted to do a picture of me kneeling behind a framed blowup of one of my *Playgirl* shots. By this time, I was getting a little sick and tired of the *Playgirl* business. I mean, what the hell! Here I've been playing my heart out for ten years at football, but that was just too mundane. It took a near-fatal injury, my posing in the raw, acting lessons, and a law degree to turn me into a hot item. To compensate, I demanded action photos of me catching a football attached to these stories with their featured *Playgirl* pictures.

That summer, I was also taking saxophone lessons. My grandpa was a great saxophonist, and I had always gotten a special charge out of hearing him play. I grew up loving the instrument and the sound of an alto sax. Having never done anything musical in my life, I started saxophone lessons with a motivating fantasy of me looking out of a picture window at the lights of San Francisco Bay while playing the sax. It was like a magazine ad for brandy.

During that off-season, I was saddened to learn that our receiver coach, Lou Erber, had quit and was now coaching for the New England Patriots. He phoned me before he went east to say that he was sorry to leave me and believed I had a couple of great years left in me. His replacement was a thirty-two-year-old who was, if you can believe it, younger than I was. He turned out to be the total opposite of Lou, whom I had grown so fond of over that two-year period.

Meeting Tom Walsh for the first time in minicamp, I saw that he was a real rah-rah textbook coach who had never played football—not a mandatory requirement, mind you (he had been a baseball player in his day)—yet knew a lot about football because he studied it conscientiously. A real goodie-two-shoes, the guy was married and refused to stay out at night, never wanted to go to the bars, didn't drink, didn't smoke—and worst of all, saw no justification for the rest of us doing any of those things. At first, I really resented his ordering me around and making me do certain drills that were utterly senseless. I mean, the guy was acting like a damn college coach. He told us how poorly we'd played the past season and how we had let our patterns disintegrate. And he persisted in calling me "old man," until I suggested to him after practice one day that if there was any sporting event he thought he could beat me in, to step forward and give it a try—and then we would see who the real old man was. Amazingly, you could tell him to fuck off, and the very next day he'd come back totally unaware that you were ever mad at him. No one threw him or could even penetrate this man. I grew to admire him because he was so damn consistent. And he genuinely cared about improving everyone's performance, regardless of what you had accomplished in the past.

I came home from minicamp feeling very depressed. With this new coach, meetings and practice would end up being twice as long. I also got the distinct feeling that Walsh favored younger players who were easier to control. I was getting crotchety like any old veteran, yet I still felt that I deserved a little respect. I did things my way because these habits had kept me playing well for eleven years. It was too late to change.

I worked out with weights like a madman that off-season in order to knock Coach Walsh's socks off with my newfound strength. But I never got the chance to flex those muscles—not even once.

10

A Striking Season—What Am I Gonna Do When I Grow Up?

Between minicamp and returning to training camp in Santa Rosa in mid-July 1982, Marilyn and I bought and moved into the house of our dreams. It was magnificent and contained everything we'd always wanted in a house. Located in the hills of Montecito overlooking Santa Barbara, it was a two-hour drive from Los Angeles. Away from the smog and overbuilt urban ugliness of Los Angeles, Marilyn, Marisa and I had found our Nirvana in this place, which cost me close to half a million dollars. What the hell! I'd taken a lot of punishment over the past twelve years, and now it was time to start enjoying the fruits of my bone-crushing labor. We enrolled Marisa in a phenomenal private school which she adored, and Marilyn was so happy in these serene surroundings that she even began thinking seriously about having another child. Whatever fears I may have had about tying up all of our liquid assets in the down payment and being saddled with a gigantic mortgage, I pushed away, knowing that my earning capacity for the next couple of seasons would comfortably cover the costs.

Despite my excitement and appreciation of our new home and life-style, I must confess that my attitude was less than spectacular when I got to training camp in Santa Rosa that July. I was beginning my twelfth year in the NFL, and having had six receiver coaches and five head coaches, I just was not as mentally attuned to Walsh's regimen as I should have been. I mean, at this stage of my career, I felt that I didn't need to be treated like a rookie. Walsh was unbelievable. He'd run five miles between practice sessions and then would stay up till 1:00 A.M. studying films after our meetings. After a refreshing six hours of sleep, he'd come to morning practice screaming, yelling and jumping around. Meanwhile, the veterans would go out for a couple of beers before curfew and then watch TV till about 2:00 A.M., and we'd pay the price the next morning. Now, I've always been incredibly moody in the mornings; even Marilyn can't deal with me until noon. It was at those morning sessions that I found Tom's personality to be the most abrasive. I kept thinking that I'd done too much to have to put up with this crap. Objectively, football is never based on what you have done in the past, but what can you do *now*? I figured that Walsh thought my playing potential was behind me.

Besides me, Walsh was very tough on Cliff Branch, a top wide receiver who was going into the eleventh year of his career. Branch had had a terrible season the year before due to some personal problems, and it seemed as if Tom had a mission to bring Cliff back to his former days of glory. Instead of trying to befriend Cliff and take him aside to talk to him, Tom would say some obnoxious things to him during our meetings such as, "Hey, Cliff, wake up for Christ's sake," or, "Where's your god-damned playbook, Cliff, is it still under your pillow? You can't learn this stuff by osmosis!" I figured that Cliff had been through too much to have to take this kind of shit in front of his teammates. Walsh didn't have a lot of empathy when it came to handling and dealing with the players.

During the first few weeks of training camp, I was always operating at about three-quarter speed. The meetings after practice in Lou Erber's era of being our coach were short and intensive. Each coach usually has his own way of explaining things, but in reality all of the plays are fairly similar. I mean, you can only run so many patterns, and there are only so many kinds of defense. It becomes a semantic situation, since different coaches will relate things in different ways. This season we were adding to our offense by putting in the short passing game, a three-step drop by the quarterback that puts quick pressure on the defense. Naturally, we had to learn some new terminology that Walsh gave to these patterns, but the nightly meetings dragged on and on. He was anxious to do his job right, but the repetition really got to me. Tom justified the long meetings because we had so many young receivers. But in the back of Tom's mind, I'm sure, was the fact that the longer we met, the more likely we wouldn't be out carousing at the bars, which was probably true.

Tom Walsh's greatest quality was his consistency. Whether he was consistently an asshole or not was beside the point. His biggest fault was that he was young and lacked experience dealing with professional athletes. But Tom Walsh was smart and he cared. He cared very much about improving everyone's performance, no matter how competent that player already was. Had I not felt so discouraged about myself and my leg, I think Tom and I would have become very good friends.

I guess I'd reached a point where I felt like I was in limbo regarding football. I couldn't concentrate at the meetings or on the practice field. I missed the camaraderie I had with Lou Erber which made each practice session tolerable. I had become very picky and hard to work with because I felt a lot of what I was doing in training camp was a waste of time. I was doing drills that I just didn't think were useful. Tom would put us through sideline catching drills. Now, if there was one thing that I did better than anyone in the NFL, it had to be catching the ball on the sidelines. It aggravated me that this guy would coach me at this and treat me as if I'd never done it before. The drill had to be done, but there was no reason to try and coach me at it. He had a coaching point to make regarding everything I did. It gradually became a joke among my teammates. Hendricks or Rod Martin, or any one of the other defensive players, would watch me doing drills and then say, "Hey, Chandler, can't you do anything right?" or "When are you going to learn how to run an out?" I really resented Walsh's coaching, and not because I didn't need it, but primarily because I was not receptive to it.

Dwayne Osteen, a defensive back, was a guy that I had run against in practice many times. I got used to running against him when we both worked out at the Rams' practice field during the off-season. Being a real competitive guy, Dwayne could sometimes become too competitive and often start fights. Now, he was beating the hell out of some of our young receivers, mainly trying to intimidate them. Just after the ball was thrown, he would jam the guys when he didn't need to and would push them around. Ordinarily, I never spoke much at our nightly meetings, but one night I got a little upset while we were watching films of that day's practice. I spoke out saying that the receivers should fight back at the defensive backs—when he jams you, you should hit him back, or when he goes for your throat while you are running your pattern, you've got to go for his throat. I was pissed because Dwayne was out there trying to intimidate and hurt guys in practice. These were his own teammates, and there was no reason to injure them or make them look bad so that he could show what a tough guy he was in practice. The guys at the meeting that night were very surprised to hear such pointed remarks coming out of me, primarily because I'm not a tough guy. I can take a lot of blows, but I'm not so great at giving them out. The following day, I ran an out-and-up against Dwayne, who went for the out move, so I beat him pretty bad on the up. I was wide open, but the wind was blowing against the quarterback, who threw the ball too high in the air, which caused me to have to wait for it. Dwayne was running as fast as he could to catch up while I was waiting for the ball. When I caught it, he tackled me and spun me to the ground, which knocked the shit out of my elbow. Lying on the ground for a few seconds, I thought that this was exactly what I was telling them not to take the night before. I got up and had to swing at Dwayne. Fights during practice are never frowned upon, since they kind of fire up the team. However, the coaches tend to break up fights with wide receivers to make sure that the receivers don't break their hands.

Even though we didn't fight very long, it really felt pretty good to get into hand-to-hand combat and take out some of my frustrations. What surprised Dwayne was that I had been lifting weights with Matt Millen (ha, ha), our 255-pound linebacker, who could bench-press over 500 pounds. I was actually getting bigger—not big enough to scare anyone, mind you, but nevertheless, bigger. The next day, Dwayne and I were talking as usual. Fights in pro ball rarely go beyond a day. Nobody carries grudges. When the fight is over, it *is* over! There is no residual hostility left on the field. Tempers run high and there's a tremendous amount of competitive pressure, but guys know that everybody is doing the best he can to cope with it.

At our next practice, we were running inside-twenty-yard-line passes. Even though I was no longer upset with Dwayne, I was still feeling very competitive and wanted to beat his ass pretty good. I was over on the left side in a slot formation. Dwayne was the outside corner playing me head up about seven yards off the ball. I was running a comeback and tried to make too radical a cut. The instant I planted and torqued, I felt my leg snap, and I lay on the ground in excruciating pain. I was afraid to look at it for fear that it had snapped in two.

When the pain subsided, I managed to get to my feet and stagger off the field and into the locker room with George Anderson, our trainer. Even though I wasn't sure what exactly was wrong with my right knee, I became devastated psychologically. Having had four surgeries on my left knee, I always considered my right leg and knee as a pillar of strength. It was the only completely sound leg I had left, and it had always compensated for the perpetual problems of the left leg. Sitting on the training table, I got very emotional and began crying quietly. I couldn't erase from my mind the moment that leg snapped. For months after that I would cringe and get goose bumps when I relived that moment. Nagging thoughts filled my head about the fact that this might end my season and possibly my career.

When George said he thought it might just be a strained ligament, I desperately wanted to believe him. Rod Martin looked at
it, and he also said it didn't seem to be too serious an injury. As
much as I wanted to believe them, I knew in my heart from that
awful snapping sound that something was seriously wrong.
George then went out onto the field to tell Al Davis that he
thought everything was going to be okay. A few moments later,
George returned to see if I would be willing to go back out onto
the field. Al Davis had asked if I would jog around the field just
to let my teammates know that I was okay. A deep feeling of
despair set in upon hearing this request. Instinctively, I knew I
was badly hurt despite the other opinions. And now, I was asked
to swallow that fear and help keep up the morale of the team. I
couldn't force myself to make that token appearance.

Instead, I went back to my motel room and sprawled out on
the bed. After the sun went down, I just lay there in the dark, my
knee packed in ice, thinking that it was all over for me. How
could I have been so careless as to let this happen to me at the
very beginning of the season? If there was ever a moment I
wanted to have back, it was right before this injury. I knew I
could have prevented it.

The next day, I got all the radiation I wanted from the battery
of x-rays on my knee. The pictures showed there were no broken
bones, and my regimen was to just rest my leg for about five
days, icing it down regularly and seeing how it felt.

By the twelfth day, I was lifting and running and started to do
more out on the field. After the regular practice, which I did not
participate in, I grabbed a quarterback and had him throw me
some ups. On about the seventh one I jumped and came down
awkwardly on my knee. The leg buckled and snapped again. I
didn't get up this time because I saw Al Davis and Tom Flores
talking on the edge of the practice field. I lay there, making it
look like I was just resting, for about twenty minutes until I saw
them leave. I just didn't want them to see that I couldn't walk,
because I wasn't ready to accept that yet.

That night I limped onto a plane for Los Angeles, and the next day I saw a doctor in my hometown of Whittier, who drew some fluid out of my knee. His diagnosis was that I had merely stretched the lateral collateral ligament of the knee, which wasn't devastating but would take three or four weeks to heal. He said what I wanted him to say, but I still don't think I believed him.

Going back to the Bay Area, I rested the knee for ten days and noticed no real improvement. I finally told Dr. Fink that I was heading back to LA to have a doctor set up an arthroscope for my knee. I went to see Dr. Norman Sprague, one of the finest in the business and very conservative. After examining my leg in Los Angeles, he said he feared I had torn my anterior cruciate ligament and possibly the cartilage. If he reconstructed the anterior cruciate, I'd never play football again. So we decided to do arthroscopic surgery to confirm his diagnosis and do what he could with the scope. Knowing that I'd change my mind if I thought about it any longer, I took a taxi to the hospital where Sprague was to meet me. During that cab ride, I had an eerie feeling that this was the beginning of the end.

Upon learning how uncomfortable I had become about general anesthesia, Sprague agreed to give me an epidural, which numbs you from the waist down and leaves you awake during the surgery. He got into the knee and saw that the cruciate ligament had snapped just as he had feared. He snipped the torn ends out of the way so they wouldn't catch in the joint and trimmed the edge of the cartilage. I had hoped this might work, but it turned out to be a false hope.

The first time I worked out after the surgery, my knee just slid out again. I tried every knee brace in the country, but none actually prevented the problem from occurring. Back in the Bay Area, I kept trying to build up my leg while the Raiders played the first two games of the season and won without me!

Then came the strike. Although they had been trying to negotiate before the NFL players' contract expired, a new contract had not been hammered out in time. We all felt that the strike wouldn't last more than two weeks. After all, the team owners would lose a helluva lot more than the players. But what we didn't realize is that they could afford to lose a helluva lot more. The old contract gave the players about 30 percent–35 percent of the gross income derived from the twenty-eight teams. Now, we were striking to take advantage of the bigger television dollars and percentages of pay TV. The players now demanded 55 percent of the owners' gross income, which would be distributed to the players on a seniority basis. Even though this would have doubled my salary, I was philosophically opposed to this socialistic concept. I still felt that all players should be paid, and be able to negotiate, according to their abilities and not just because they had lasted the longest in the NFL.

After four weeks had elapsed, all of us players were becoming very frustrated. I went back to Santa Barbara, but I couldn't relax because my right leg was still shaky, and I kept worrying about the salary I was losing every week. After driving Marilyn crazy for a while, I returned to Oakland to wait it out and step up my workout program.

I spoke with the players' representative almost daily and even had a few conversations with Al Davis. Mind you, I wasn't pro management because I thought the owners hadn't offered us anything worthwhile; however, I knew that Al Davis was busy recruiting the other team owners to lay out a viable offer just to begin the bargaining process and get this thing over with. Every team in the NFL was divided between those who were for the strike and those who opposed it. By the eighth week of the strike, it appeared that the entire season was in jeopardy. The next two weeks were crucial, with both sides eager to get on with the sport of football. At long last, we ratified a new contract which was nowhere near what we originally asked for. But the good news was that we were going to get paid again. As part of the settlement, veteran players with over six years in the NFL would receive $60,000 as career-adjustment pay. Now knowing that I could meet my current obligations, I headed back to San Francisco feeling that we won the best deal under the circumstances. But I was also frightened about the team's expectations of me. I had led the coaches to believe that I was in great shape to play because that's what *I* wanted to believe. My leg was strong, but it still was unstable.

I didn't play for the first two weeks of our resumed season. Tom Walsh kept asking me to tell him when I thought I was ready. Everyone was putting up with me, and I liked having my own rehabilitation schedule again. But I wasn't being productive for the Raiders. The team was playing very well. We were winning all of our games. The Bay Area sportswriters were all saying how nice it would be to get Bob Chandler back on the field again. I secretly feared that old Bob Chandler would never really be back again. I remained on a list where the team could make you active or inactive each week. No one had made the final decision to put me on injured reserve. After three weeks of inactivity, Al asked me how I was feeling. When I replied that things just don't feel good, Al didn't get upset. He just said, "Hang in there and get it strong, and maybe you can help us down the stretch." At moments, I felt good, but I would then get depressed because I knew I was going to end up letting him down. Deep down, I knew that I really wasn't the same anymore.

We were about to play Seattle, and I told Tom that I could play with my knee brace if I stayed low and kept my knee bent in a flexed position. It felt funny to run my patterns so low, but Walsh had enough faith in my ability to send me in during the second quarter. This was the first time I had played all year. When I got in the huddle, all the guys ribbed me by saying, "Who is this guy?" But it still felt great. The first play that I went in motion was to the left away from Marcus Allen, who ran the ball off right tackle. I crossed back across the field and threw a key block—a great block—allowing Allen to run about sixty yards and be tackled on the three-yard line. As I was coming off the field, half the guys on the team were putting their arms around me and congratulating me like I had scored a winning touchdown. I was terribly moved, as it felt so wonderful to once again be appreciated by my peers. And I knew they were pulling for me to come back. Subconsciously, I think players love seeing another player come back from a serious injury because it reinforces their belief that they would be able to do the same if it ever happened to them. Later in the quarter, I ran a corner pattern, and when I tried to make a sharp cut to the outside, my leg slipped out again.

Whatever false hopes I had about being back to normal just disintegrated again. During the next week's practice, the coaches were expecting me to play more, but I knew that I was getting worse.

Before the strike, the deal had been set for us to become the Los Angeles Raiders. Since so many of the players already had homes and apartments in the Bay Area, we continued practicing in Oakland and would fly down to our home games in the LA Coliseum. We became the only team in the history of the NFL to be a road team every game. Because the season was so short, I was staying at the Oakland Hilton, where I was paying a special rate of $900 a month. I grew to hate the place and moved to an apartment at 1000 Chestnut, in the Russian Hill area of San Francisco, that our kicker, and my friend, Chris Bahr, had found. The rent for this really snazzy apartment was $1400 a month. After a couple of sleepless nights, I realized that I was crazy spending this kind of money and got my deposit back. I moved into the Oakland Hyatt, which gave me a better rate than the Hilton.

The reason I was feeling so uneasy about spending money was that I had just been notified of something by the team's accountant which threw me into a state of shock. It seemed that for the first two games before the strike, I earned $12,500 based on my adjusted $100,000 yearly salary. However, I was taxed as if I was making $200,000 a year, since I had already been advanced half my salary to buy my house. Thus, out of the $12,500, I had only cleared $4,000. Then I learned that the $60,000 we veterans were supposed to get in that career-adjustment pay wasn't going to come until January 2. So I had no money coming in from that either. And believe me, I had some hefty bills to pay. I was slowly running out of ready cash to live on. Now this accountant-type guy informed me that according to his records, I made $12,500 before the strike, and I lost $87,500 during the strike, which comes to $100,000. And since the team advanced me $100,000 before the season, I was told that I wouldn't be getting any more paychecks for the balance of the season. Something was wrong with this picture! I hoped.

The team had done me a big favor by advancing me the $100,000. Al did it as a favor to me. No one really figured that the strike would materialize. Anyway, I had agreed to be paid $100,000 during the year. What they should have done was to have continued paying me $6,250 a week for the remainder of the season, and then at the end of the year, or anytime before that, come to me saying that I owed them whatever portion of the $100,000 I had lost during the strike. Then it would have been my obligation at that time to pay them what they overpaid me. Instead, they made this unilateral decision to stop paying me, period!

Furiously, I went to Steve Ortmeyer, a coach who also had administrative duties, and argued that this was handled very poorly and insisted they shouldn't have gone about collecting their money the way they did.

Two weeks went by, and there was no change made. I approached Steve again, who told me he'd speak to Al again. Al told him to tell me that things were very tight at that time, and Al just didn't have the extra money. The pressure of not being able to get out from under was too much, and I think I reached my breaking point. Sitting in one of Tom Walsh's meetings, all of these financial horrors were filling my mind. I knew that I really couldn't play, and felt like I was financially wiped out. I abruptly got up, walked out of the meeting, drove over to the Hyatt, and just stayed in my room. I don't remember if I pulled the covers of the bed over my eyes.

Talk about reaching the lowest point imaginable, I knew I couldn't handle any more. I called Marilyn, who asked what I was doing. I replied that I was in my hotel room. She said, "Aren't you supposed to be at practice?" I told her that I wasn't going to practice. What does it matter now? They can't fine me since I don't get any paychecks. Marilyn tried to commiserate with me, but said that I had to regroup and handle this setback better than I was. I yelled a few obscenities at her, trying to explain that there was nothing I could do. I felt I was no longer able to summon the composure and strength to handle the situation.

So I lay there for two hours, and it was getting closer to three o'clock practice. It dawned on me that I was doing the easy thing by running away. It was my obligation to get to practice. So, in a mindless state, off I went to practice where I just sat on the sideline, since my leg wasn't worth a damn and I was tired of faking it. I fantasized that management would approach me, saying that they were genuinely concerned about the fact I wasn't getting paid. They must've had more pressing matters on their minds. Finally, later that day, Al walked up to me and asked me what I needed. He said, "Just tell me what you need to live on until you get your $60,000 from the league." I told him that I didn't want to be obligated to him for anything more. He had already done me a big favor by advancing me the money for my house.

The very next day, Al lent me $50,000, which he said he'd take out of the career-adjustment money. I now was able to breathe a little easier and regroup.

But all of my dreams had crumbled by this time. I phoned Marilyn to tell her that we were going to have to simplify our lives. My career was over. We would have to sell the house, which she had worked so hard to fix up. And Marisa would have to leave the private school that she loved so much. And to complicate matters, Marilyn had just found out that she was pregnant. For the first time in my life, I felt like one of those guys who play for years and years and ultimately crawl away from the game with nothing. It was almost funny how fast my fortunes had turned. I mean, I wasn't broke, but all my assets were tied up in property out of which I couldn't squeeze ready money. My life was predicated on making a certain amount of money to meet my heavy expenses. I had finally done what I swore I'd never do—

extend myself to the breaking point. Everything fell apart for me on that day in August when my knee went down.

I had ignored the warning signals and fallen into the biggest trap facing any professional athlete. As the money gets bigger, so does the life-style, and it all can disappear in an instant, with one injury.

My bills were mounting. Never thinking that I could get injured, I had fantasized making a smooth transition retiring from football into being a highly paid broadcaster without missing a beat. I felt particularly lousy about having exposed Marilyn to all these fancy toys and now having to cut everything back.

At any rate, despite my monetary difficulties, the entire Raiders' staff was expecting me to play because I had been giving them signals that I was healing. We were in Cincinnati, which has a stadium with artificial turf. Flores wondered if my playing on the artificial crap would worsen my condition. Now, I knew that my knee was not going to feel any better, so I had some Xylocaine injected into my knee for our Saturday practice, to see if that made a difference. I knew the risks involved, but again, I felt that I was letting the team down by not trying this one last thing. Al had done me another big favor by advancing me the money, and I owed him one. I wore my leg brace, and with a totally numb knee, I went out on the artificial turf on Saturday and felt absolutely great. I ran through all my patterns and was about 90 percent of my capacity. Within four hours, however, the Xylocaine wore off, and the knee was in excruciating pain. It was so sore the next day that I couldn't even put on my brace. I had to tell Flores that I couldn't play, as I didn't want to take another shot of local anesthetic. Yet, I told him that if something happened to one of the receivers, I would go in. It was a ridiculous statement, since my knee wasn't worth a shit, and they knew it.

Flying back to the coast from Cincinnati, I started facing one of my life's biggest problems. For over a decade, I had always been able to handle the beating and injuries to my body. Now, for the first time, I was unable to handle my injury. My dogmatic faith in the medical profession was shaken because nothing had helped my problem. I wondered if I had finally reached a point in my life where I could no longer heal, or had an injury that ultimately couldn't be fixed.

On our way back to Oakland that night Dr. Rosenfeld and I talked for about an hour about what could possibly be done to improve the knee. He advised me that there was the possibility that my cartilage was more torn than Dr. Sprague had diagnosed. For the first time, I learned that there is a technique where the surgeon can shore up the outside of the knee without having to go into the entire knee joint.

In the meantime, Rosenfeld wanted me to wear s sturdier leg brace. I mean, this new brace was no Ace bandage wrapped around the limb. This was a metal and plastic brace used for severely handicapped people. No other wide receiver in the history of the game had ever worn one of these contraptions. But it really did nothing to change my condition other than hampering my speed and agility. At practice sessions, I still kept deluding myself that this new brace would eventually help me because I knew Al Davis was getting impatient about when I was going to be able to play a little.

We flew to Kansas City the next week where I told the coaches that I would hold for field goals and extra points. On the first field goal attempt, Chris Bahr missed a short one, and I began thinking that the coaches would start second-guessing my ability to hold, notwithstanding that I'd been a field goal holder for eleven years. On the next field goal, the ball was blocked and bounced right behind us. I got up to start chasing the ball before they could get it, and my knee buckled just as badly as it ever had. I crawled off the field and told Dr. Fink that I was through.

Back from Kansas City, I told the Raiders' front office that I'd decided to go in for surgery. I told them that I wanted to go to LA to see a doctor for the Rams who had performed this type of surgery on a number of players. Flying down the next day, I was lucky that Dr. Shields could fit me into his schedule. After his examination, Dr. Shields explained the procedure that was necessary to restore my right knee. Opening it up, the surgeon would pull the hamstring muscle down and around on both sides; then he would sew the muscle into the bone in front, which would stabilize the entire joint. The best part was that he would not have to go inside the knee joint itself. I then asked him if he could perform this surgery under an epidural. Ordinarily he wouldn't, he said, but when he saw how paranoid I'd become about a general anesthetic, he agreed, saying that as long as my hamstring muscle stayed very relaxed, it would be okay. I told Dr. Shields that I was not concerned about playing football again (seems like I'd said this once before), all I wanted to do was be able to ski or play golf and be active with my family.

Shields wanted me to have the surgery soon, so I would be all healed by the time minicamp took place in May. He felt strongly that I should at least have the option of football, since he was certain that the operation would help me considerably. And psychologically, it would be much more advantageous to have Al Davis see me running in May rather than waiting until July's training camp.

I still asked Shields to postpone the surgery until after the season. For years I'd been trying to get an invitation to play in the Crosby Pro-Am Golf Tournament at Pebble Beach, and the week before my appointment with Shields, I received a personal invitation from Nathaniel Crosby to enter the tournament. The tournament was February 1, and I just wanted to wait two months so I could play in it. Shields thought I had to be crazy to put off the surgery because of some golf game. He was absolutely right. Why should I give up the option of playing next season, especially if my other choices like broadcasting didn't work out?

I flew back to Oakland trying to figure out how I could alleviate a very touchy situation. When I told Dr. Fink about my decision to have Shields operate, he said there might be a problem because they would want their own surgeon, Dr. Rosenfeld, to handle the surgery. Dr. Fink told me to ask Al. Next, I told Tom Flores that I needed the surgery quickly. He was saddened that this marked the end of their hopes for my comeback. It was mid-December. He too told me to talk to Al.

I was in the locker room that afternoon lifting weights when

Al came in to get his rain gear. It was pouring and the wind was damn near fifty miles per hour. I said, "Al, can I speak to you for a moment?"

He said, "Yeah," and kept on walking out toward the field. I was wearing shorts, so I had to hurry to pull some sweats on and quickly follow him out on the field, like a little puppy following his master. He stopped and started watching the practice, and I told him about Dr. Shields' diagnosis and that I needed to have the surgery the next week in order to have a chance of being ready for next year. So I was literally begging him to put me on injured reserve. Davis said he'd feel better if our own team doctor was doing it, and he added that he hoped I would be available until the end of the season, just in case. I put forth my sad tale once more while Al was staring out at the field. He then said, "Goddamnit, I hate to have that happen."

I looked up feeling grateful that Al was so sympathetic toward me and said, "Don't worry about me, Al. I'll be okay. I only have to wear a cast for six weeks."

Davis replied, "I wasn't talking about that. Malcolm just dropped the ball."

I thought, Jesus, here's my whole career at stake, and he's more interested in Malcolm dropping the ball. I muttered, "Okay, I'll be down at the Centinella Hospital in LA next Thursday in case anyone is looking for me." I walked off, upset and confused.

Al then grabbed me, saying, "No, wait, Bob. I'm sorry I can't give you the time you need, but practice just isn't going well." It had just started five minutes ago!

I nodded and he said to keep in touch. I walked away thinking how crazy this profession was. It wasn't Al's fault, and he meant nothing personal by his remarks. It was merely that I was no longer a productive piece of machinery for him, and he was worried about a big game coming up.

Feeling very sorry for myself, I went back to the locker room and just threw all of my equipment into my locker, packed my bags and flew down to Santa Barbara to wait until Thursday.

Marilyn drove me down to LA, and after getting my epidural,

Dr. Shields was ready to perform his miraculous surgery on me. The anesthesiologist had given me such a large amount of anesthetic that I didn't regain any feeling in my legs for about ten hours after the surgery.

My folks saw me in the recovery room, and I barely had the strength to talk to them. From the look in my mother's eyes, I could see her asking me how much more punishment I was going to inflict on myself.

The hospital was fantastic to me because Dr. Shields had instructed them to roll out the red carpet. Marilyn was able to stay over, and the next night, which was New Year's Eve, they set up a table with a candle and a bottle of wine right in my room.

As I was about to check out of the hospital, I caught the flu and began throwing up, which kept me back in the hospital for three days longer.

Staying in Santa Barbara to recuperate, I still drove down to Los Angeles to watch the remaining regular season game and the two playoff games. I would swing my cast over toward the passenger seat and accelerate and brake with my left foot. I needed to sit with the guys on the bench during those last few games because I knew that this might be my swan song season. I suppose I was happy that I could at least maneuver about on crutches instead of being in a wheelchair. But no matter how hard I tried, I just didn't feel a part of the team. I kept thinking of myself as an outcast.

Driving back to Santa Barbara, where my house was up for sale, I thought about the past twelve years. I broke out into a sweat thinking of some of my bone-crushing, on-the-job injuries. Was it all worth it? Was it worth giving up my spleen, having nine surgeries, breaking bones the way most people break toothpicks, and suffering the agony of having Xylocaine wear off as games ended?

Still, there was all that adulation of the fans. I smiled as I drove my Toyota northward on Route 101. Why was I now driving a Toyota? During my last week in Oakland, I was having dinner with some of the Raiders in a restaurant. A disgruntled fan was upset about the players and the team leaving Oakland. So he kicked in the side of my Mercedes and jumped up and down on the hood. My car had $3,000 worth of damage and needed a total paint job. So I rented a Toyota while my car was being repaired. It was almost poetic that my career had ended almost as inconspicuous and unassuming as it had started. Back to basics, I thought as I watched the fog blowing in across the highway. Despite the gray atmosphere, I was feeling relatively happy. The football profession is strictly a day-to-day proposition. Who knows? Maybe my leg will heal entirely. And maybe I'll get one more season before I'm through.

EPILOGUE

In the end, I was completely spent.
No longer could I summon forth the mental strength to quiet
* the fears and accept the punishment.*
Questions had become real, and that reality was a dead-end street.
To understand that something I loved so much was destroying
* me was the only pain I couldn't overcome.*

—BOB CHANDLER
1983—Los Angeles, California

That off-season before I retired, I worked out religiously to get that leg in shape. After all, I had always been able to come back before.

The surgery done by Dr. Shields was very successful, and I was feeling pretty good. My workout routine took place every day under the guidance of Gary Tuthill, my good friend who also happened to be the trainer for the Los Angeles Rams.

I put off running any patterns or really testing my knee until the last minute. With three weeks before the start of the 1983 season, I figured I had better try. Before running my first pass route, I was as "nervous as a long-tailed cat in a room full of rocking chairs." The running patterns went okay, but there was something missing. I wasn't ready to admit it, but I had lost the quickness and recklessness that had made me special. I needed to find someone who would tell me that everything was okay, and the leg was just another mental barrier that had to be overcome. So I went back to Dr. Shields.

He was very optimistic, saying that everything looked good and I should give it a go. Despite his encouragement, I still had serious doubts. In actuality, I may've been looking for someone to tell me, "Bob, it's all over, but that's all right because all good things must end sometime."

My last stop before making a final decision was at the office of Dr. Norman Sprague, the physician who'd originally diagnosed my problem. Dr. Sprague also said that things looked fine under the circumstances, adding that he felt I could probably play one or two more years without any serious problems, but he couldn't give me a guarantee. It suddenly hit me that nothing in this life is guaranteed, so why was I trying so hard to get some facsimile hammered out? Sprague finally said, "You're asking tissue to do something that it wasn't designed to do. But, I tell you one thing, Bobby, if you do damage that knee one more time, there's a good chance you'll never get it back to the way it is now." As I left his office, Dr. Sprague wished me luck and admitted that he'd love to see me play again if that was what I really wanted.

Walking to my car, I thought to myself, "All right, Chandler, you're back to square one. There's no one who can make this decision for you. What's it gonna be?" I paused on the street and stared at a bunch of Little League kids going through batting practice on an empty lot. God almighty, they were having such a good time. Baseball for them was still a wondrous game, and they looked eager enough to want to spend a great part of their lives playing this game. I thought of myself at that age when my friends and I would toss the football around in somebody's backyard. My eyes were slightly glazed as I walked over to a pay phone and called Marilyn. When she answered, I said, "I've decided to retire." She couldn't quite believe her ears, but she knew that a decision like this hadn't come easily and would've only been made if it was definitely the right time.

I walked out of the phone booth and took a deep breath. So here it was, the moment every professional player knows is inevitable. It's just that no one knows how to handle it until it happens. Not feeling like driving right away, I just kept walking down the street in this unfamiliar neighborhood. A few minutes later, I spied a small tavern, went in, and ordered a beer. It was my first beer as a non-football player. The beer tasted the same, but I was different. I had lost my security blanket and felt that I was being forced to grow up fast.

My decision was finalized four days later at a Raiders' golf tournament. I had had a funny feeling for some time that the Raiders had some real doubts about my physical well-being. After all I had been through, the one thing that would have killed me was having the Raiders tell me to forget it and not come to training camp. All players want to leave on their own terms, but very few ever really get the chance.

Having always had the fantasy of my being able to say good-bye in a dignified way rather than having the team telling me to leave, I decided to seize the opportunity. In the golf clubhouse, I saw Tom Flores coming down a corridor toward me. Before he could say a word, I blurted out, "Tom, I'm retiring. The leg's not good enough for me to play at the level that I'm used to."

Tom replied, "Bobby, are you absolutely sure?"

"Without a doubt," I said, "I've been a pretty good ballplayer, and I want to be remembered that way."

Tom gave me his blessing, thanked me for all that I'd done, and wished me luck. That was it.

The next few months, I had lots of doubt and second-guessing. Life without football was much more difficult than I had ever imagined. I never realized that I enjoyed the game so much until I no longer had it. No matter how much you think you've prepared for the end, the reality is unbearably hard. I found that one of the worst adjustments was accepting that a very important physical part of my life was over. No longer could I run and jump and exhibit those special God-given talents I was always grateful for.

During this adjustment period, I was fortunate enough to procure the services of Ed Hookstratten, the entertainment and sports attorney. Ed had known me from Whittier, where we had both grown up. He was willing to take on this not-so-old but worn-out football player and help him become a sports broadcaster. Hookstratten arranged my meeting with Ted Nathanson, the coordinating producer of NBC football. They decided to bring me on board as one of their new color commentators.

Of course, I was no longer twenty-one years old and feeling indestructible. Once you've quit the game, I mean finally shut the door, you've lost your reason to convince yourself that physically everything feels good, which was what kept you going from week to week.

Life was so secure under that helmet. It was all I had ever known. The roller coaster ride had become a way of life. But as with every professional athlete, the time had come to strip away the armor, leaving a vulnerability from which to grow.

Yep, I'd come full circle. Here I am a rookie again, not knowing what to expect in this field, but I'm confident and waiting for a chance to prove myself all over again.